THE JOHN HARVARD LIBRARY

The John Harvard Library, founded in 1959, publishes essential American writings, including novels, poetry, memoirs, criticism, and works of social and political history, representing all periods, from the beginning of settlement in America to the twenty-first century. The purpose of The John Harvard Library is to make these works available to scholars and general readers in affordable, authoritative editions.

SELECTED POEMS OF FREDERICK GODDARD TUCKERMAN

EDITED BY BEN MAZER
INTRODUCTION BY STEPHEN BURT

JOHN
HARVARD
LIBRARY

THE BELKNAP PRESS OF HARVARD UNIVERSITY PRESS

Cambridge, Massachusetts, and London, England   2010

Library of Congress Cataloging-in-Publication Data

Tuckerman, Frederick Goddard, 1821–1873.
[Selections. 2010]
Selected poems of Frederick Goddard Tuckerman /
edited by Ben Mazer ; introduction by Stephen Burt.
p.   cm.—(The John Harvard Library.)
Includes bibliographical references.
ISBN 978-0-674-05048-8 (cloth : alk. paper)
1. Nature—Poetry.   I. Mazer, Ben.   II. Title.
PS3104.T5A6   2010
811.′3—dc22   2009044557

Contents

SELECTED POEMS OF FREDERICK GODDARD TUCKERMAN

Introduction

In January 1855 the most famous poet in the English-speaking world prepared to receive yet one more obscure visitor, one of hundreds each year who made the trek (boat and train rides, then two and a half miles, usually on foot) to Alfred Lord Tennyson's home on the Isle of Wight.[1] Tennyson welcomed friends, but grew weary of strangers, and he was not partial to Americans. But this American was different: Frederick Goddard Tuckerman of Greenfield, Massachusetts, demonstrated his great knowledge not just of Tennyson's work but of English verse generally. They seem to have talked poetry all day. Tennyson wrote to Tuckerman afterward: "That you past [sic] your three days here happily is another satisfaction to me; for the place is dull enough . . . so your happiness must have been derived from your talks with myself over my little fire in my wind-shaken attic." Their few surviving letters discuss meter and elision, and make clear that the American read aloud to the British Poet Laureate Tuckerman's

own then-unpublished poems. The poets also traded pipes; Tucker-
man later sent Tennyson Noah Webster's *Dictionary,* and Tennyson
gave Tuckerman the manuscript of "Locksley Hall." Tennyson con-
cluded his letter with the "hope that if ever you come back to us you
will put up at no hotel but in my house, and if I come to you [I] will
likewise find you out."[2] Though that return visit never took place, the
Tennyson household remembered the first one well enough for Em-
ily, Alfred's wife, to send a note of condolence to Tuckerman's sister
after the American poet died.

Tuckerman in 1855 was unknown for good reason; he had pub-
lished a handful of poems in New York magazines, but no book,
and nothing that gave him more than the adjective "promising"
even among his influential acquaintances. And they were influential
(Ralph Waldo Emerson was one); Tuckerman came from a promi-
nent Boston family, and lived in or near Boston (he attended Harvard
but did not graduate) until 1847, when he moved to Greenfield. Nor is
Tuckerman a household name today. Over the century plus since his
death, though, it has become clear that the gifts Tennyson found in
the man were gifts he put into the verse, and especially into the verse
he wrote after the misfortune that defined his later life—the death of
his wife, Hannah (sometimes called Anna), in 1857, shortly after she
gave birth to their third child.

Tuckerman had a superb ear, a sense of the music in a pentameter
line, rare in any country or century. He had, too, a sensitive, and an
unflinching, attention to the psychology of mourning; and he made a
strenuous and a reflective attempt to reconcile his melancholy tem-
perament with religious faith. Tennyson's own poems had those vir-
tues too; a few modern critics have called Tuckerman (it is genuine
praise) "the American Tennyson." But Tuckerman's poems do other
things that his English friend did not do, and did not try to do. He
showed his technique in a panoply of sonnets whose variety expanded

the limits of the fourteen-line form. He did so as a poet of New England, of its landscapes, its local history ("Wassahoale" and "sagamore George"), and especially its plant life: he became an American poet of natural history, the American poet who best records the failure of the great nineteenth-century enterprise called natural theology. The Tuckerman of the sonnet series looks into himself, looks at the mullein's golden stalks and at the ocean's crests and troughs, looks for evidence of a just God there, and discovers—perhaps without ever having read Darwin—that such evidence is not to be found.

Tuckerman had *Poems* (1860) privately printed, sending it to writers he admired, among them Emerson (who liked "Rhotruda"), Longfellow, Hawthorne, Tennyson, and Jones Very, his former tutor at Harvard. A double sonnet from *Poems* (not part of the sequences) appeared in the *Atlantic* in 1862, and other New England magazines reprinted it. The intricate poem enumerates beauties in nature—

> The starry flower, the flower-like stars that fade
> And brighten with the daylight and the dark,—
> The bluet in the green I faintly mark,
> And glimmering crags with laurel overlaid,

and then concludes that all these evidence a divine hand, "ultimate atoms of one infinite Ball / On which God moves, and treads." It was a claim his sequences of sonnets would come to question, if not to reject.

A British firm republished *Poems* commercially in 1863; the book was picked up by one leading U.S. publisher, Ticknor and Fields, in 1864, and reprinted by another in 1869. Tuckerman, or someone close to him, cut out and pasted into a notebook all the reactions to his verse that he could find. Reviewers compared him to Tennyson and, oddly, to the master of Victorian vers de societé, W. M. Praed; they praised his powers of observation but also called his syntax, and his use of form, obscure. English readers noticed American settings: "he has evidently been familiar," wrote *John Bull,* "with Nature in the back-woods." His sonnets, said the New York journal *Round Table,* "violate all the known laws of that artificial species of verse." The *London Review* singled out "The starry flower" as incomprehensible. The same sonnet attracted American parodists. The Springfield *Republican* published "A sonnet—After F. G. T":

> The cloudy style, the verbal mist that floats
> And glooms between the daylight and the dark—
> The book, whose choicest lines we never mark,
> The laurel, poisonous to nibbling goats . . .

Tuckerman pasted that into his notebook too. The *Atlantic* itself admired his poems of "bereavement and sorrow," and his detail-work: "The trees, the shrubs, the flowers of New England are known to him as they are to few." The *New York Times* agreed: its reviewer was glad "to find a poet who knows just how the laurel disengages its corolla, who knows of coltsfoot, monkshood and pearlwort . . . Mr. Tuckerman," the *Times* added, "is said to be a personal friend of Tennyson, and his poems are somewhat Tennysonian."[3]

The town of Greenfield had Tuckerman compose an ode for the dedication of its Civil War monument in 1870; for the half century following Tuckerman's death, residents of Greenfield who remembered the ceremony were almost the only readers that Tuckerman had. The essayist Walter Pritchard Eaton, however, praised Tuckerman as "a forgotten American poet" in 1909, recommending his "tender, wistful and scrupulously accurate contemplation of the New England countryside," "his golden bursts of imaginative vigor, his wistful contemplative melancholy, his disregard of academic form."[4] Eaton saw only the 1864 book, which held only, among the sequences, the First and Second Series; Sonnets, Third, Fourth, and Fifth Series, appeared in print only in Witter Bynner's edition of 1931, and "The Cricket" only in 1950.

Those years began a Tuckerman revival—modest in its effects, intemperate in its claims. The Stanford University poet and critic Yvor Winters, a stern opponent of modernism, championed Tuckerman in the 1950s and 1960s; the last edition of Tuckerman before the present one, N. Scott Momaday's, was prepared at Stanford under Winters's direction. Tuckerman's restless intellect, his self-doubt, his sometime piety, and his attention to natural history became for Winters and his intellectual allies proof against Romantic faith in a boundless self: "Tuckerman's Anglican orthodoxy and his scientific naturalism," writes one such ally, "kept him clear of the Emersonian error."[5] Such arguments have not won, for his self-scrutiny, and for his superb ear, the attention that they deserve.

Most of Tuckerman's best poems are sonnets, and most of the sonnets come to us in the five "Series" that he arranged. These sonnets begin as expressions of grief at the death of Tuckerman's wife, and they return to that subject as birds to their winter home ground; behind them lies the structure, and the all but unassuageable sadness, of Tennyson's *In Memoriam A. H. H.* (1850).[6] Like the British laureate, Tuckerman wrote of "Life, Love, Experience, Art,/ Fused into grief" (II:XII). Tuckerman became at once a student of grief and a student of botany, seeking at once leafy detail for its own sake (he always finds it) and evidence of God's plan for us (which he does not find): the groves and waves, the ferns and the constellations he watched so often and so avidly reveal patterns we can record, but no benevolent, humanly comprehensible purpose. This poet of grief and of natural history is also our first dedicated American poet of the disenchanted, inhuman biosphere: as much as his rhetoric belongs to his era, as much as he does retain a Christian faith, he seems at times closer to *Nature*, the scientific journal, than to Wordsworth's Nature (which "never did betray/ The heart that loved her"), or to Emerson's "Nature," with its "radical correspondence between visible things and human thoughts."[7]

Some readers imagine Tuckerman as a man who became a recluse, and therefore devoted himself to natural history, after the love of his life passed away. But Tuckerman did not simply turn to nature after he lost his wife; he had an eye for it, the sonnets say, in "schoolboy-days," when "the eye that shrank from hated hours . . . Knew each bleached alder-root that plashed across / The bubbling brook, and every mass of moss" (II:XXIX). Tuckerman's journal, begun after his move to Greenfield, starts with astronomical data, but turns its attention quickly to botany; he would make entries in a herbarium until 1868. A narrative poem from the 1850s directs its humor at an unworldly, melancholy New England poet who could be the author himself:

> Full well he knew the stars and flowers,
>   The atmosphere, its height and pressure,
> The laws that gird the globe, and powers
>   That make our peril or our pleasure.
> He knew each bird, its range and sphere;
>   For plant and shrub, had many an odd use:
> But naught of farming-growths or gear,
>   And less of garden-sauce and produce.

Tuckerman's life coincided with what the English journalist Lynn Barber calls (it is her title) *The Heyday of Natural History, 1820–1870*. In those years British and American amateurs studied and practiced botany, geology, and animal taxonomy in unparalleled numbers. Harvard students founded a Society for Natural History in 1837, Tuckerman's first year there.[8] Amateur naturalists, in America as in Britain, justified their pursuits by the doctrine called natural theology: "the more we learn to understand and appreciate Design in Nature, the more closely we approach a knowledge of God."[9] "Nature was the work of God's thought," explains the modern critic Christoph Irmscher; "Change . . . was merely the revelation, the unfolding of an underlying essence."[10] It was a doctrine unstable even before Darwin, since the study of nature—in Tuckerman's case, of weather, coast-lines, and forestry—brought so much evidence of violent flux. (Con-sider Tuckerman's opening line: "And Change, with hurried hand, has swept these scenes . . ." [II:XVIII].) In Tuckerman's best poems natural theology, the claim that we can know God through an or-dered nature, becomes inseparable from a mourner's theodicy, the at-tempt to get past personal loss by proving that God's ways are after all just.

The sequences show both projects together as both approach the point of collapse. Tuckerman's poetry dramatizes, again and again, the exhilarating and frightening discovery that nonhuman nature is not like us and not like our inherited notions of God. Other nineteenth-century writers made such discoveries after reading con-troversies about geology, or (from 1859) after reading *The Origin of Species;* Tuckerman at least sounds as if he made them by watching the weather, the plants, the seashore. So, at times, does *In Memoriam:* "Are God and Nature then at strife?" It was a question that occurred to Tennyson, but it preoccupied Tuckerman, who seems to have spent so much time exploring the woods. The question would unsettle more than just orthodox Christian beliefs; it contradicted, too, the Romantic ideas by which "all beings are thus derived from and ex-pressive of an original ideal unity . . . evident in the network of corre-spondences that pervades the cosmos—between the macrocosm and the earth, between the earth and the human microcosm, between plants and animals."[11] These are the correspondences that Emerson found in what he called "Nature" as well: "Tuckerman yielded up the consolations of 'correspondence,'" writes the critic Denis Donoghue, "very reluctantly, but with a scruple that he could not put by."[12] It is tempting to say that Tuckerman is to Tennyson as the mid-nineteenth-century "field naturalist" is to the "closet naturalist": the latter authoritative, prestigious, a prolific writer at the cultural center; the former more specialized, unlikely to theorize, sometimes (for better or worse) provincial, long undervalued, and better acquainted with the outdoors.

Tuckerman does not abandon natural theology willingly, nor does he abandon it all at once. Nor, I should add, does he stop believing in a God: rather, his problem—made gloriously and heartbreakingly clear in his descriptive passages—is that neither his God, nor his observations of nonhuman nature, can explain our suffering. In Emerson's "woods, we return to reason and faith. There, I feel that nothing can befall me in life . . . which nature cannot repair."[13] Tuckerman tests such claims by giving as much attention to the woods as any nineteenth-century poet except the Englishman John Clare: and, sometimes, Tuckerman finds that the claims do not hold. The double sonnet printed in the *Atlantic* insists that natural history can unify the night sky and the flecks in rocks, that the same particles must comprise, the same patterns animate them both. It also finds in those very patterns evidence for a benevolent personal God: "His hand, who touched the sod with showers of gold, / Stippled Orion on the midnight blue." Elsewhere, though, Tuckerman admits a kind of parody, or a cruel revision, of Romantic natural unity: stars are like plants and follow the same laws, fascinating to record, but they are not our laws, and cannot meet our needs. "A Soul that out of Nature's Deep" concludes that we may contemplate Nature as much as we like, we may love to do so, we may love it more than we love ourselves, but we will learn no moral law thereby:

> Too late he learned that Nature's parts
>   Whereto we lean and cling,
> Change, but as change our human hearts,
>   Nor grow by worshipping;

And that her presence, fair or grand,
    In these faint fields below,
Importeth little, seen beyond
    Our welfare, or our woe.

It is an anti-sermon, anti-Transcendental, almost resigned: "Nature" is like us, but only in being inconstant. "Nature" rewards observation by giving us more to observe, by giving us symbols, but not by giving us wisdom about human life, and in that admission it seems both chilly and modern. (Why are the fields "faint"? Because the poet stands too far above them; or, in western Massachusetts, with its high slopes and damp spring, because the field has morning fog and dew.) This particular poem collapses into glib advice ("Nor good from ill can we release,— / But weigh the world in full") but its discovery remains. The sonnets, for all their nods toward Christian orthodoxy, make the same discovery again and again, finding in that discovery reasons to rearrange, and to disarrange, sonnet form.

Tuckerman merits sustained attention not because—like thousands of other Victorians in Britain and their contemporaries in America—he questioned equations between observed patterns in nature and a putative divine law, but because he paid such attention to those patterns, and because he made them into vivid and resonant poems—above all, into sonnets. The sonnet sequences begin by asking—they never stop asking—how to connect flora and fauna to human loss and human truth, and whether that connection can even be made. "What though from every bank I drew a flower,— / Bloodroot, king-orchis, or the pearlwort pale"? "What avail / Is the swan's voice, if all the hearers fail?" The swan sings as he must (and, myth says, he must sing at his death): we cannot give a reason for his action, just as we cannot say why we write poems, or why God acts in His mysterious ways. "Depending so, / God were not God, whom knowledge cannot know" (I:I).

Tuckerman has appealed to some modern religious readers because (unlike Whitman) he says that he believes in a Christian divinity ("O Father, God!") (I:XXI): but it is a divinity that never intercedes, never comes down to earth, and never reveals evidence of a plan *for us,* much less a reason for Hannah to die. As children in Boston the poet and his sister crossed the Common and "heard with awe that left no place for doubt/ God's anger mutter in the darken'd heaven" (III:V). Such a God will not explain Himself: we have the choice, on His created Earth, to contemplate either our human loss, or the rest of His Creation, whose laws govern only itself. Even a poem that begins "O rest divine!" will not address the divine: instead, it remembers the "golden" smiles of Hannah, likening them to a peaceful brook, and likens her bad moods (he misses even their quarrels) to the beautiful oddities of a violent rain, "When the whole Shower is swinging in the wind, / And like a mighty pendulum, urg'd & driven, / Beat back & forth between the earth & sky!" (III:VII).

When Tuckerman looks around him—or even when he reads the reports of those who have looked around them, as in poems set in the Southern Hemisphere—he sees almost indecipherable complexities, beauties that demand appropriate words but that will not agree to emulate, or even to promise, justice for us. "Nature daily through her grand design / Breathes contradiction where she seems most clear" (I:XXVI). On the Argentine Pampas, the unfortunate wanderer "Sees the vault blacken, feels the dark wind strain, / Hears the dry thunder roll, and knows no rain" (I:V). Closer to home, the poet finds "Cold April flowers in the green end of June," and moments when

The night-hawk blew his horn at sunny noon;
And in the rainy midnight I have heard
The ground-sparrow's long twitter from the pine,
And the cat-bird's silver song,—the wakeful bird
That to the lighted window sings for dawn. (I:XXVI)

After we admire the detail-work (the sparrow's Keatsian "twitter," Tuckerman's note as to what tree the sparrow prefers), we can see that these are details out of place: sparrows and nighthawks can seem to break their own laws, though really their asynchronous behavior shows the variation that governs nature, that sets it apart from our human sense of desert, of a moral law. Tuckerman concludes that any God who can make the world fair, who can authorize a moral law or justify our sufferings, must not after all be available in "the round natural world," nor in "the blue abyss" of ocean and sky (I:XXVIII). Yet even as he resolves to seek that God elsewhere, his temperament keeps him here: the Earth and its creatures, its sky and its sea, are what we know, perhaps all we can know. He hopes that his soul, after death if not in prayer, might "pass to God;/Shooting the void in silence, like a bird,—/A bird that shuts his wings for better speed!" (I:XXVIII). Here if anywhere Tuckerman aspires wholeheartedly to flee from Nature, to enter the divine, a realm that he locates wholly elsewhere, wholly beyond human justice and beyond the leaves on all trees. Such moments are rare, though, and even they describe aspirations, rather than experiences. Tuckerman draws his figurative language from nature, from animal behavior, even when he is describing his restless soul.

The sonnet series are so sad, so given to indecision, so attentive to "Nature" as a source of contradiction and flux, that their irresolution has proven hard to critics—as it was hard for Tuckerman—to accept. "His true mission in life," says one scholar, "is to observe and record the workings of nature—an activity that releases him from his earlier doubts and misgivings."[14] No, it does not. Sonnet II:XXX represents a bleak parody of the Wordsworthian poet's calling: "beneath Canadian sky," and "on Long Island's void and isolate capes," the poet heard, as a boy, "the same deep dirge": it was a song he would have to channel in his own poems, once he figured out what it meant, and what it meant was simply that he would lose the woman he loved. Few poets have explored their own griefs at such depths, and few griefs have seemed, at the end of those journeys, more useless: he gets no lesson, no guidance, from his calling, just as the would-be natural theologian in Tuckerman learns, from nature, nothing to make his world whole.

Yet he continues to credit some divinity. Human life has "one end," in death, and one prescription for conduct in this world: so Tuckerman believes, and so he says, and yet he cannot concentrate on either. He is distracted, at first by his grief over a particular death, and then, in accordance with his temperament, by the variety of nonhuman life: what is death, what is right conduct, what are social demands

> to him, unto whose feverish sense
> The stars tick audibly, and the wind's low surge
> In the pine, attended, tolls, and throngs, and grows
> On the dread ear,—a thunder too profound
> For bearing,—a Niagara of sound! (I:XVII)

We can see in Tuckerman the terminus of a process that the critic Paul Fry identifies in William Wordsworth, in which the poet ceases to imitate composed music and attends instead to nature's acoustic gifts: "sound supersedes music as a poetic occasion."[15] Midway through this process we get the Aeolian harp, its strings played by the wind, to which the first Romantics compared themselves. At the end of the process, in Tuckerman, the poet can acknowledge that the scheme behind his words, assembled with human intention, differs from the laws that govern the waterfalls, the pines, the clockwork stars.

Tuckerman merits attention not just for what he sees, what he feels, and what he might believe, but for how his poems sound, and for how they connect sight and sound: "Where the black shingles slope to meet the boughs, / And—shattered on the roof like smallest snows— / The tiny petals of the mountain-ash" (I:X). The lines work by consonance (shingles, shattered, ash) but also by observation, and by a kind of visual pun: as the roof meets the trees, the built environment fades into the unbuilt, the old house into the flurry of "tiny" petals, as a coffin sinks under thrown earth. Tuckerman can also generate effects we now call Tennysonian:

> Then back I turn to hide my face in sleep,
> Again with dawn the same dull round to sweep,
> And buy, and sell, and prate, and laugh, and chide,
> As if she had not lived, or had not died. (II:XXIV)

Four lines, two couplets, all monosyllables, except the heavily ironized term "Again": days come back, rhymes return, meaningless hours return, as Hannah never will. Regular readers of Tuckerman will collect many more aural beauties, self-contained lines whose sound evokes what he has seen: "Thin little leaves of wood fern, ribb'd & tooth'd, / Long curv'd sail needles of the green pitch pine" (III:IV); "Contented too, to fade as yonder cloud / Dim fades, & as the sun fades, fades alike, like dim" (III:IX).

It is not true, though some critics say so, that Tuckerman's sonnets never repeat a rhyme scheme—both II:XVIII and II:XXIV use an initial envelope quatrain and then five couplets. It is true that Tuckerman seems not to *want* to repeat a rhyme scheme, and that he avoids established sonnet form. Tuckerman reverses or eliminates Petrarchan divisions between octave and sestet (the first eight and the last six lines); he brings back rhymes from a first quatrain into a last line, and he can feint toward, or use, or discard, the final couplet of Shakespearean form, which sums up, or undercuts, the first twelve lines. The intricate variety of schemes—which struck some reviewers as a chaos—may help prevent us now from growing bored with his forms. Yet no sonnet is good, or bad, just because it rhymes in unusual ways: we can ask how he uses the rhymes, and into what patterns they fall, and we can answer (for example) that their unpredictable patterns suggest the unpredictable patterns, answerable to their own rules and not to ours, that Tuckerman finds in the woods.

Though Tuckerman clearly planned the sonnets' order, they do not have anything like a plot. Nor, though they hint at such progress, do they finally lead the mourner (as, fitfully, *In Memoriam* leads its poet) back to society, back to life. The most important connections between one sonnet and the next create not an overarching appearance of progress, but a set of local narrative or argumentative units, two to four sonnets apiece. In the best (and the least noticed) of these inset narratives, a traveling speaker attracts a fervent audience for lectures on subjects (nature, astronomy) that he knows nothing about (V:VI–VII): Tuckerman resists the urge to correct him, and stands by, instead, amused. Sense and grammar sometimes require that we hook one sonnet onto the next: "they are gone" in II:XVI, for example, refers not to the plants named in earlier lines, but to Gertrude and Gulielma, from II:XV. By the end of the sonnet, even the traces of those sisters almost disappear, along with their house: "The glass falls from the window, part by part,/And ringeth faintly in the grassy stones" (II:XVI).

Such crumbling houses (see I:X as well) are sites of Romantic mourning, but they also belong peculiarly to New England, whose harsh winters and green summers could swallow them fast. Marit Macarthur writes that "by the late nineteenth century . . . rural New England . . . was littered with abandoned houses—perhaps the one Romantic ruin that Americans could find, and memorialize."[16] Tuckerman stands out for his attention to such features of the landscape, to the built and the unbuilt environment, and not only when compared to other writers of verse: he belongs in the line of U.S. "nature writing," where he occupies an unusual place, after Thoreau, and before such late-nineteenth-century prose writers as John Burroughs and John Muir. Burroughs's controversial essay "Nature and the Poets" (1881) called for accuracy in verse about fauna and flora, praising Whitman, Emerson, and Tennyson, who usually achieved it: "our natural history," Burroughs concludes, is "rich in materials for the poet that have hardly been touched."[17] Had he read Tuckerman, one hopes he would have admired him.

The more you know about the American wild, the more you can see what Tuckerman has done with that knowledge. "Whippoorwill-shoe, and quaint Sidesaddle-flower" exemplify the "beauty . . . seen where'er we look, / Growing alike in waste and guarded ground" (II:VIII). Tuckerman knows that pine woods use poor wet soil, that they represent the first stages of regrowth after damage (e.g., a fire), and that they are acoustic dampeners:

> Far from the roar of day, beneath your boughs
> Fresh griefs beat tranquilly, and loves and vows
> Grow green in your gray shadows, dearer far
> Even than all lovely lights, and roses, are. (I:VII)

When Tuckerman takes up Thomas Cole's famous figure, the River of Life ("As when, down some broad River dropping, we, / Day after day, behold the assuming shores"), he removes almost all the consolations of adulthood, but adds what he knows about actual rivers. The watercourse slows down and grows less picturesque as it descends, while the vegetation changes: "the mountains melt to vapors rare, / And life alone circles out flat and bare" (I:VIII).

Tuckerman was not satisfied with his own powers, as he was not satisfied by his own life. Sometimes the poet almost expects his theological needs to be met at last, his observations to turn into a vision: will this careful, reflective poet ever (he asks) find himself "Struck to the knees like Saul, one arm against / The overbearing brightness," so that he may "hear—a Voice?" (I:IX). In a word: no. He sees the Earth; he sees the (lowercase) heavens, and the constellations there. He has observations, and memories, but never visions. When Tuckerman records, as Milton did, a vision of his dead wife in a dream, it is not even his dream: rather, "a fair young mother," perhaps a neighbor, tells the widower that *she* has dreamed of Hannah (I:XXIII).

Tuckerman elsewhere sounds guilty, or apologetic, about the very close-to-the-ground temperament that gave his poems strength. Such an apology generates sonnet II:VII, in which the poet whose "brain/Wandered at will among the fiery stars" compares himself nonetheless to a "cunning florist" (the word could mean "flower expert" or "flower vendor") who "talked of tan and bone-dust, cutworms, grubs,/As though all Nature held no higher strain." Indeed, the poem locates the poet's heart (as opposed to his brain) right there, among the "turf, and flower-tubs" (II:VII). That sonnet plays with its unusual recurring rhymes as if to enmesh the poet himself in that garden: it rhymes *abbabccdaedecd*. We cannot divide octave from sestet, poet from florist, the psyche (whatever its aspirations) from cutworms and "shrubs."

Anyone who knows the Pioneer Valley—its striking alternations of steep forested slopes and valleys with gentle farmland, its avid greens, its summer mists, its snows—will see how well Tuckerman knew it. He also contemplates the beach and the sea. (A few of the later sonnets exist in draft as a separate group called "Long Island.") Fleeing the house and the city they remember, the poems move back and forth between the forests around Greenfield and the Long Island shore; both are at once places of vitality and gravesites, and neither admits of permanent alteration by human hands. Both fascinate; neither one compensates for human loss, unless indeed we lose ourselves in it. One of Tuckerman's best sea sonnets portrays him

> As one who sails, a landsman on the deep,
> And, longing for the land, day after day
> Sees the horizon rise and fall, and feels
> His heart die out,—still riding restlessly
> Between the sailing cloud, and the seasick sea. (II:XXII)

The rise and swell of matching consonants—first l's, then d's and f's, then finally sibilants—matches the unlikely sailor's feelings, trapped on a sea that does not cease to change. As good as his eye for New England seems to have been, Tuckerman could also evoke places he could not possibly have seen: "Like those vast weeds that off d'Acunha's isle / Wash with the surf, & flap their mighty fronds . . . Yet cannot be disrupted from their deeps / By the whole heave & settle of the sea" (IV:VIII). (Tristan da Cunha, an archipelago in the south Atlantic, is today the most remote inhabited place on Earth: it features in Poe's *Narrative of Arthur Gordon Pym*, though Tuckerman must have found the seaweed elsewhere.)

Nature, Burroughs admits, has "definite meanings and laws," "powers and economies," but they are not the laws recorded by poets, who instead record "what it provokes in [their] own soul"—this even though Burroughs asked that they get their facts right.[18] We cannot ask a nineteenth-century poet (we might not want to ask a twentieth-century poet) to see nature as wholly other, unusable even as a source of symbols (though John Ruskin's famous attack on the "pathetic fallacy" has sometimes been taken to do so). Rather, we can ask the poet (as Burroughs did) to describe it well, and to distinguish between nature's laws and our minds even while finding symbols for himself too. So Tuckerman does: his poems are full of signs for that distinction, and for his own particular distance, both from other people (after Hannah's death) and from the ways of the Earth. Tuckerman describes an Atlantic islet, a "desolate rock with lichens rusted over / Hoar with salt sleet, & chalkings of the birds" (III:X). "Rusted" because the lichens are russet (dark red) and because it suggests old age (and yet endures), the rock is another self-portrait. So is the tree cracked, killed, and discolored by lightning, "Red-ripen'd to the heart: shedding its leaves / And autumn sadness on the dim spring day" (V:XVI).

"Nature tantalizes Tuckerman," David Seed concludes, "in hinting at hidden truths and then blocking access to those truths when he recognizes the non-human autonomy of natural things."[19] The Tuckerman of the first two sets of sonnets (those he could publish in 1860; those he presumably wrote first) shows his frustration that the forests and the tides reveal no comprehensible way to a benevolent God (only to one whom "knowledge cannot know"). He, or the part of him that he calls "Grief" (II:IV), cannot find what he seeks when he looks at wild nature, though he looks and looks nevertheless: for grief, "the mountain-side may flower or flow;/Alike to that dull eye, the wild brook fills/With mist the chasm, or feeds the fields below." Grief, personified, does not care if the land burns or drowns. But Tuckerman cares: otherwise he would not record the effects of dew, of rain, of rising streams, with such attention. The later sonnets (those left in notebooks at his death) show how he permits himself to care: he can turn to the woodlands and without apology say, and show, what details he sees. By the last sequence (it is not something Tuckerman could have said in the first two), "The sky heav'd over our faint heads is heaven" (V:IV). It is the only heaven the living can know.

Tuckerman seems to have lived in relative isolation even before his wife passed away: afterward, though he had young children to care for, reputation made him "a virtual hermit."[20] Reputation, and lack of documentation, may mislead—he may have visited Boston without leaving records, and the grandees of Greenfield presumably knew where to find him when they asked him for a war poem. Yet the poems themselves speak of their poet as isolated by temperament, and (as opposed to Thoreau's writings, for example), isolation is not a state they recommend. Instead, Tuckerman says that he feels guilty about the separation from society, the immersion in nonhuman life, that his character almost demands: what good are "Life, sunlight, leisure, if they fail to urge/Me to due motion, or myself to merge/With the onward stream"? (I:XI). "Conscience" (II:XXVI) says to Tuckerman, as it said to Longfellow, not "Make your peace with God," but "Let us, then, be up and doing": the poet felt obligations to society, to other human beings, that he could not bring himself to follow. Even the sonnets hold sermons he gave to himself: "pray thy God to give . . . Some work to be by thee with reverence wrought: / Some trumpet note obey'd, some good fight fought" (IV:IV). This sonnet implies that such prayer may never be answered.

Yet Tuckerman is not only a poet of solitude, of lost love, and of natural history; he is also a poet of the U.S. Civil War, in which (like Longfellow) he wished both for a Union victory and for an end to bloodshed. When Tuckerman envisions other people elsewhere, in groups, they are sometimes the armies of the Civil War—"Men marching slow in orderly review," whose "bayonets flash, as, wheeling from the sun, / Rank after rank give fire" (I:XXV). No wonder he turns back from their perilous spectacle to the vivid memory of an unpeopled beach: "there, the wet sands shine, / And just awash, the low reef lifts its line" (I:XXV). New England's sometimes violent history has, for Tuckerman, villains and victims and martyrs, but no successful heroes: only "the Indian file" vacating the land, "the Tory priest declaiming, fierce and fat," the farmers who took up arms in Shays's rebellion (II:XIX). Virtue accomplished lies instead in domestic, familial tasks. It comes as a relief to find, in the manuscript sonnets, Tuckerman's son, "My little boy, symbolling eternity, / Like the god Brahma with his toe in his mouth" (V:III).

"Let me give something!" the last sonnets implore: Tuckerman sometimes hoped, like Longfellow, that his poetry might be of use. Yet he could not identify his own projects, nor the projects of natural history, with the projects of technology, the turning of knowledge into "Use alone": "towns, cables, cars & ships" represent the "results" that practical-minded, entrepreneurial, charitable, extroverted Americans advocate, while Tuckerman, like it or not, represents the impractical: "I in dim green meadows lean & lag" (V:V). (Why "dim"? They are covered with dew: he has come there early in the morning, or lingered through the evening.) Science and poetry stand as one for the *otium* the poet would preserve—though he feels guilty because he wants to preserve it.

"Let me give something!"—what could he give, and to whom? When Tuckerman—after the publication, and the commercial failure, of *Poems*—thinks about what he has already written, when he writes sonnets of self-evaluation, he compares himself to Tennyson, whose masterwork of private sadness became (seventeen years after he started to write it) a public success and a balm to the bereaved: "Yet some, from dire distress,/Accounting tears no loss, and grief no crime,/Have gleaned up gold, and made their walk sublime" (II:XXVII). The American *wants* to complete the arc of *In Memoriam*, to return himself and his future readers to familial concord: to turn grief into gold, if not into treasure in heaven. But Tuckerman, "poor wanderer," will not: his sonnets predict, for themselves, no such public success. One of the last sonnets also holds his last self-portrait:

> in his thought should be
> Some power of wind, some drenching of the sea;
> Some drift of stars across a darkling coast.
> Imagination, Insight, Memory, Awe,
> And dear New England nature first & last! (V:XV)

The same sonnet adds that his "end was high, whose work was well-begun": if his "end" (goal) was only observation, crystallized and made memorable, then he might have said that his work was done. But his work, as he saw it, involved finding help for grief, moral instruction, some way to get from natural observation to a "peace that passeth understanding," as the last line of the same sonnet (quoting Paul's Epistle to the Philippians) says: Tuckerman concludes that he has "almost" (but not quite) accomplished that end.

Nor did his writing come to a clear end. Multiple manuscript copies of "The Cricket" (see the Note on the Text in this volume) suggest that Tuckerman finished that ambitious formal ode near the end of his life. Winters called "The Cricket" "the greatest poem in English of [its] century," and it has attracted formidable admirers since: this formal ode may seem, to twenty-first-century tastes, over-elaborate, or imitative of Keats, in ways that are no advance on its English models, though it certainly commands respect.[21] The ode looks back on the land- and seascapes that stuck in his imagination, and then looks, or rather listens, to the nonhuman sounds of the cricket whose "song," "Ancient as light, returning like the years," promises knowledge that human beings can never have: more accurately it promises nonknowledge, a cricket's instinctive, consistent way of life, a state of nonhuman being that, for us, would be death. The cricket's song is— what Fry says poetry is too—a kind of "ostensive hum," a noise whose meaning is merely that things exist, that creatures inhabit the Earth, before they can have any meaning to convey: that they have patterns and laws of their own.

Tuckerman was no Whitman, no Dickinson, no Wordsworth; he could not have started, and never remotely wanted to start, a revolution in poetry, in its styles or in its subjects. Nor did Tuckerman— like Longfellow, like Tennyson—capture the ear and the spirit of his own age. (Dickinson, too, examined "New England nature," just a few miles away; there is no evidence that the two ever met.) The most ambitious claims that have been made for Tuckerman (Winters's, in particular) are more against other American poets than for him; he deserves to be remembered instead for what he did well. His best poems sound wonderful; he saw his cherished environments as few poets have. He presents the convolutions and the powers a poet can find in long grief, and his attention to natural detail connects his private grief to one of the great, sad movements of nineteenth-century thought, a movement he represents as no other American could. Our own time places particular value on nature writing, on "green" thinking, on writers who try to take natural processes for what they are; we seek "ecopoets" whose "topophiliac devotion" shows a "deep humility with regard to . . . nonhuman nature," and Tuckerman—more than any other nineteenth-century American—fulfills those goals within and through the workings of his poems, whose command of syntax and sound alone would be enough to set him apart.[22] Even outside New England, and long after the controversies of his own day, these are reasons enough to discover all he could do.

Notes

1. Robert Bernard Martin, *Tennyson: The Unquiet Heart* (Oxford: Oxford University Press, 1980), pp. 39, 379.

2. Alfred, Lord Tennyson to Frederick Goddard Tuckerman, Feb. 6, 1855; Houghton Library, Harvard University.

3. Notebook, Frederick Goddard Tuckerman papers, Houghton Library, Harvard University; excerpts are labeled by source, but carry no dates.

4. Walter Pritchard Eaton, *Penguins Persons and Peppermints* (Boston: W. A. Wilde, 1922), pp. 55, 63.

5. Eugene England, *Beyond Romanticism: Tuckerman's Life and Poetry* (Provo, Utah: Brigham Young University Press, 1991), p. 202.

6. Bits of Tennyson's other famous poems ("Ulysses," for example) echo throughout Tuckerman's work: sonnet I:XI, writes the critic David Seed, "comes so close to 'Ulysses' that it amounts . . . to pastiche." David Seed, "Alone with God and Nature," in *Nineteenth-Century American Poetry*, ed. A. Robert Lee (Totowa, N.J.: Barnes and Noble, 1985), 166–191: 182.

7. Ralph Waldo Emerson, *Nature, Addresses, and Lectures*, ed. R. Spiller and A. Ferguson (Cambridge, Mass.: Harvard University Press, 1979), p. 18. We should not rest with a caricature of Emerson, whose later essays, such as "Experience," admit much more doubt, and more of tragedy, than "Nature" alone contains; it is the early Emerson of "Nature" whose claims Tuckerman's sonnets reject, and who makes a foil for Tuckerman's powers—a foil that Tuckerman may have had in mind.

8. W. M. Smallwood, *Natural History and the American Mind* (New York: Columbia University Press, 1941), p. 309. Though Harvard offered

courses in botany during Tuckerman's time there, serious interest in natural history among the Harvard faculty began with the arrival of Asa Gray in 1842. Edward Tuckerman, the poet's brother, became part of Gray's "team of experts" on expeditions; Edward, who taught at Amherst College, not far from Greenfield, would become an authority on American lichens. A. Hunter Dupree, *Asa Gray* (Cambridge, Mass.: Harvard University Press, 1959), pp. 107, 172, 351.

9. Lynn Barber, *The Heyday of Natural History, 1820–1870* (London: Jonathan Cape, 1980), p. 23.

10. Christoph Irmscher, *The Poetics of Natural History: From John Bartram to William James* (New Brunswick, N.J.: Rutgers University Press, 1999), p. 240. Irmscher is writing not about amateur naturalists' beliefs, but about the beliefs of Louis Agassiz, the paleontologist, taxonomist, and anti-Darwinist who came to Harvard—like Gray—after Tuckerman left: it is natural theology, all the same.

11. Nicholas Jardine, "Naturphilosophie and the kingdoms of nature," in *Cultures of Natural History*, ed. N. Jardine, J. A. Secord, and E. C. Spary (Cambridge: Cambridge University Press, 1997), pp. 230–248: 233.

12. Denis Donoghue, *Connoisseurs of Chaos* (New York: Columbia University Press, 1984), p. 62.

13. Emerson, *Nature, Addresses, and Lectures*, p. 10.

14. Donald Stauffer, *A Short History of American Poetry* (New York: Dutton, 1974), p. 118.

15. Paul Fry, *A Defense of Poetry* (Stanford, Calif.: Stanford University Press, 1995), p. 45.

16. Marit MacArthur, *The American Landscape in the Poetry of Frost, Bishop and Ashbery: The House Abandoned* (New York: Palgrave Macmillan, 2008), p. 12.

17. John Burroughs, *Pepacton* (New York: Riverside, 1895), p. 109.

18. Ibid., p. 113.

19. Seed, p. 188.

20. Samuel Golden, *Frederick Goddard Tuckerman* (New York: Twayne, 1966), p. 47.

21. Frederick Goddard Tuckerman, *Complete Poems,* ed. N. Scott Momaday, with a preface by Yvor Winters (New York: Oxford University Press, 1965), p. xvi.

22. J. Scott Bryson, *The West Side of Any Mountain* (Iowa City: University of Iowa Press, 2002), pp. 4, 12.

Note on the Text

The extant body of textual material facing any editor of Frederick Goddard Tuckerman's poetry consists chiefly of a large collection of autograph manuscripts, which are housed at the Houghton Library at Harvard University, and the four editions of *Poems*—1860 (Boston: privately printed by John Wilson and Son), 1863 (London: Smith, Elder and Co.), 1864 (Boston: Ticknor and Fields), and 1869 (Boston: Little, Brown and Co.)—that were published in Tuckerman's lifetime. The extant manuscripts contain versions of all of the poems published in *Poems*, as well as a large body of other poems, in both cases often in multiple versions. Some of these manuscript materials discernibly represent fair copy versions of poems, for example in the case of an entire notebook which was apparently intended for use by the printer who set the first edition of *Poems*. Others represent drafts of poems, sometimes fragmentary in nature. In addition to these materials, not many more than a dozen of Tuckerman's poems are known to have appeared in literary periodicals during his life, and in one or two instances in ephemera connected with public ceremonies.

The first edition of *Poems* was privately printed, presumably at Tuckerman's own expense, and undoubtedly with the design that it should launch the reputation of Tuckerman's poetry in the literary society of the time. A list he kept tells us that Tuckerman sent copies of this edition to Tennyson, Emerson, Hawthorne, Longfellow, William Cullen Bryant, George Ripley, Jones Very, Charles Frederick Briggs, James T. Fields, George S. Hillard, and other literary figures. The three subsequent editions, though issued at different times by three distinguished commercial publishing houses of the period, one of them English, are in most respects typographically identical to each other, so that in a sense they represent a single edition, with relatively few textual changes distinguishing them from the privately printed edition of 1860. The 1864 Ticknor and Fields edition is rendered distinct by the presence of an errata slip not included with the other editions, and by a single change in punctuation (1864 has a comma after "grief" at the end of line 2 of Sonnet II:XXVII, where 1863 and 1869 have a colon). It is upon the presence of this errata slip that the particular authority of the 1864 edition in comparison with the other editions turns. The errata slip (recording ten changes in wording only) provides us with Tuckerman's latest corrections for the published text of *Poems* and supplies us with evidence of authorial approval of the edition as a whole, once the corrections which it dictates have been rendered.

The differences between the 1860 text and that of 1864, which shall be understood to include the corrections called for by the errata slip, are relatively few. Between the 1860 edition and the 1864 edition, there are not many more than two dozen differences in wording, in seventeen of the one hundred poems represented. There are twenty-nine changes in punctuation, occurring in eighteen poems. There are, additionally, nine changes in the spelling of a word, two changes of case, four changes involving apostrophes, one change involving abbreviation, one change involving indentation, and one change involving a stanza break. Altogether there are forty-two poems which in the later editions contain changes of any kind whatsoever.

Poems was reissued by Little, Brown in Boston in 1869 in an edition which was printed without an errata slip or corresponding changes to the text, and which did not include the single punctuation change made in 1864. The 1869 edition is textually identical to the 1863 edition. Samuel A. Golden conjectured that Tuckerman may have been "completely unaware of its printing" (Golden, 1966, 43).

A common observation of Tuckerman scholars and editors has been that Tuckerman's punctuation in the manuscripts appears to have been provisional. It is frequently arbitrary, sometimes nonsensical, and, in the poems that exist in multiple versions, inconsistent from one version to another. The punctuation of the first edition of *Poems* does not follow that of the fair copy notebook apparently intended for use by the printer who set that volume. Tuckerman appears to have expected someone other than himself to punctuate his poems for publication, and it is traditional in Tuckerman scholarship to assume that someone other than Tuckerman was responsible for the punctuation of the published editions of *Poems*. (It was not uncommon at the period for poets of reputation to expect their work to be punctuated by a house editor; Byron, for example, is known to have allowed house editors to repunctuate his texts.)

What no Tuckerman scholar or editor has noticed is that the printer who was hired to privately print the first edition of *Poems*— John Wilson of Boston, formerly of Glasgow, Scotland—was the author of a *Treatise on Grammatical Punctuation* (Manchester, U.K.: printed by the author, 1844), revised as *A Treatise on English Punctuation* (Boston: printed by the author, 1850), which was issued in more than twenty editions.* It is my proposal that Wilson was responsible for the punctuation of the text of the 1860 edition of *Poems*.

There were few changes in punctuation from the 1860 edition to subsequent editions of *Poems*. The errata slip which accompanied the 1864 Ticknor and Fields edition exists as evidence that Tuckerman approved of its mild emendation of Wilson's punctuation.

At the Houghton Library at Harvard University, there is a copy of *Poems* marked "Imperfect Copy" which was believed by Eugene England and Jonathan Bean to be an ordinary copy of the 1860 edition of *Poems*, with authorial corrections marked in it in pencil by Tuckerman. It has gone unnoticed that this copy of *Poems* contains more than 420 individual differences in wording, punctuation, or spelling from the ordinary 1860 printing. The binding is the same as that of the regular issue. I propose that this unique copy of *Poems* was produced by Wilson as a bound proof from which Tuckerman made final corrections prior to the printing of the standard edition of 1860. The bulk of the corrections marked in the "Imperfect Copy" are changes which were incorporated into the 1860 edition of *Poems*. These handwritten corrections include nearly every one of the thirty-five changes in wording included in the final printing. Twenty-six of the printed wordings which were changed are consistent with wordings in MS Am 1349 (2), the fair copy notebook of *Poems*. The remaining nine differences in wording represent what must be considered an intermediate stage in the development of the text of *Poems*.

The rest of the changes made in the final printing are almost entirely changes in punctuation—many of them consisting of the addi-

---

* Itself an expansion and revision of portions of *The Text-Book* (Belfast: Simms and M'Intyre, 1826), the authorship of which was attributed to "a compositor"— subsequently republished, with revisions, as *The Compositor's Text-Book* (Glasgow: Richard Griffin and Co., 1848) by "John Graham."

tion of commas or the revision of commas to a heavier mark such as
the semicolon—only three of which are marked in pencil by Tucker-
man in the "Imperfect Copy." The bound proof reveals that (1) Tuck-
erman took meticulous care in his revisions, (2) stages in the commu-
nication of changes between author and printer of the 1860 edition
of *Poems* (probably one or more revised proofs) are missing, and (3)
Tuckerman was intimately involved with the printer in arranging the
text of the 1860 edition of *Poems*. Implicit in the revelation that he
made meticulous changes in the wording of his text between the
proofs of 1860 and the edition of 1860 is Tuckerman's approval of the
punctuation of the 1860 edition of *Poems,* whether he had a hand in
the final punctuation or whether John Wilson was entirely responsi-
ble for this. The existence of a prepublication proof of the 1860 edi-
tion of *Poems* is strong evidence that the final printing was approved
by the author, despite the fact that he felt compelled to make further
wording changes in subsequent editions.

N. Scott Momaday, whose edition of *The Complete Poems of Fred-
erick Goddard Tuckerman* was published by Oxford University Press
in 1965, chose the manuscripts at the Houghton Library for his copy-
text for the poems which Tuckerman published in his lifetime, ignor-
ing evidence that Tuckerman subsequently communicated changes to
his editors. Momaday's text contains misreadings and liberal inter-
ventions in punctuation, and there are blatant instances of rewriting
of poems in manuscript—in many cases Momaday's text duplicates
errors or interventions found in Witter Bynner's seminal edition of
The Sonnets of Frederick Goddard Tuckerman (New York: Alfred A.
Knopf, 1931). (There are numerous instances of rewriting of Tucker-
man's sonnets by Bynner, sometimes though not always for the sake
of meter, but it might be pointed out that such editorial practice was
not uncommon at the time—Robert Bridges, for example, changed
wordings in Gerard Manley Hopkins, and Emily Dickinson's poems

were sometimes rewritten by her early editors.) Jonathan Bean's se-
lection of Tuckerman, in *Three American Poets: Melville, Tuckerman
and Robinson* (London: Penguin Books, 2003), sought to redress pre-
vious editors' reliance upon the manuscripts and to use as its copy-
text, where it covered the material, what seemed to be the best text,
that of the 1864 edition of *Poems,* incorporating the corrections item-
ized in the errata slip. While correcting many of Bynner's and Mo-
maday's misreadings, particularly in poems for which there exist only
manuscript sources, Bean's edition introduced its own misreadings
as well as numerous interventions in punctuation and other acci-
dentals.

The John Harvard Library Edition

Where it covers the material, this edition presents the text of the 1864
edition of *Poems,* incorporating the corrections called for by the er-
rata slip. The errata slip is strong evidence that the text of 1864, when
corrected to incorporate its changes, represents the author's latest ap-
proved version of the text, and the only commercially published ver-
sion bearing evidence of authorial approval. Three individual copies
of the 1860 edition of *Poems,* with authorial changes marked in pencil
(nearly all of which were incorporated into the 1864 edition of *Po-
ems*), survive in the collections of Columbia University, the Univer-
sity of Chicago, and the Greenfield Historical Society. Given the evi-
dence of authorial approval for the edition of 1864, and working on
the assumption that Tuckerman marked these corrections at some
stage before the commercial editions appeared, rather than late in life,
it seems unlikely that the changes that Tuckerman marked in copies
of the 1860 edition should supersede the authority of the text of 1864.
All of the poems in this present edition from "November" through
the second of the sonnet series (eighty-six of the one hundred poems

in *Poems*) are given precisely as they appeared in the 1864 edition of *Poems*.

In the case of poems for which there exist only manuscript sources, I have provided those versions which evidence suggests are the latest and most finished. I have preserved Tuckerman's punctuation and other accidentals as they appear in the manuscripts. The third, fourth, and fifth sonnet series are provided here in the fair copy versions—for the majority of these sonnets the only versions—comprising the entirety of the notebook MS Am 1349 (5), which, relevantly or not, is dated "Greenfield Dec, 1872." "Ode. for the Greenfield Soldiers Monument," "The Shore," "An Incident," and "The Cricket" (about which more below) are given in the versions which appear in MS Am 1349 (4), a notebook which Tuckerman used for recording fair copies of finished poems. The combined force of two pieces of evidence constitutes the basis for my belief that MS Am 1349 (4) was a notebook which Tuckerman was filling with fair copies of finished poems at the time of his death. One of these is a note in Tuckerman's hand, written next to the poem "The Incident" in that notebook, and dateable to within three months prior to Tuckerman's death. It reads: "This poem was sent to the Springfield Rep. Feb 7th / 73 but has not appeared." In addition, analysis of the word changes from version to version in all the manuscript versions of poems which appear in MS Am 1349 (4) gives the strong impression that the versions in MS Am 1349 (4) are uniformly the latest and most finished.

This is the first edition to print a manuscript poem previously unnoticed by Tuckerman scholarship, titled "Twilight" (but unrelated to the poem of the same name which appeared in *Poems*). This poem is legibly written in Tuckerman's hand in the notebook MS Am 1349 (3), which otherwise contains drafts in whole or in part of numerous poems included in *Poems*, but also of poems which appear to have been composed subsequent to the publication of that collection (including several of the presumably late sonnets). It is given here precisely as it is worded and punctuated in MS Am 1349 (3).

This is also the first edition to print a single authoritative text of "The Cricket," without resorting to the creation of a "composite" version drawing upon variants of wording or punctuation present in other of the five extant versions, and without otherwise subjecting the text to forms of intrusive alteration.

"The Cricket" is known to have existed in five separate undated manuscript versions. There are minor variants in wording and greater inconsistencies in punctuation which make each version distinct. Momaday, who was aware of only four of the five versions, believed that "Cricket 4" (as he so dubbed one of the two versions in MS Am 1349 [7]) was the latest and superior version. He ignored the likelihood that MS 1349 (4), in which "Cricket 2" (printed in this edition) appears, is a fair copy notebook which Tuckerman was filling with finished versions of poems immediately prior to his death. But even though he found "Cricket 4" to be superior, Momaday took liberties in borrowing variants in wording present in other versions of the poem. In his punctuation of the poem, Momaday hardly followed "Cricket 4" at all, or indeed any one of the versions. Consequently, he did not provide a text of "The Cricket" which is based upon the authority of a single version of the poem.

In editing "The Cricket" for his Penguin selection, Jonathan Bean rightly chose "Cricket 2" as his copy-text, but imposed more than fifty changes in punctuation and allowed himself the freedom of selecting alternative word choices from the other versions. Of the six readings which are unique to "Cricket 2," Bean in fact used only one, "laugh and blush" for "tittering blush" in line 60; otherwise his wording is not different from that of "Cricket 5."

The Cummington Press's 1950 edition of "The Cricket" (whose unnamed editor was the printer Harry Duncan) used a sole version of the poem (the early draft "Cricket 1"), but introduced three changes in punctuation and one misreading ("layster's" for "Caÿster's" in line 67). After the book had gone to press, Duncan saw Samuel A. Golden's photostatic copy of "Cricket 5," as a result of which the Press produced an "N. B." listing the variants in wording found in "Cricket 5," without identifying the source of the variants. When the *Massachusetts Review* published "The Cricket" in 1960, Mordecai Marcus incorporated these variants, reconstructing the wording but not the punctuation of "Cricket 5."

The source for the incomplete poem "Poesy" is a letter from Tuckerman to his brother Edward, dated January 1, 1852, and preserved in Houghton Library MS Am 1349 (7). Although the poem is not given in its entirety in the letter, Momaday was able to provide only the first eighteen lines of this poem (in an appendix in his edition), not having seen both pages of the letter, one of which had been placed in the Houghton Autograph File. Eugene England printed an inaccurate transcription of the twenty-seven lines given in the full letter, in *Beyond Romanticism: Tuckerman's Life and Poetry* (Provo, Utah: Brigham Young University Press, 1990). Here in the John Harvard Library edition these lines are printed correctly for the first time.

Ben Mazer

Chronology of Frederick Goddard Tuckerman's Life

1821   Born on February 4 at family homestead in Bowdoin Square area of Boston.

1825   Tuckerman family moves to 33 Beacon Street in Boston.

?   Briefly enrolls in Episcopalian private school of Bishop John Henry Hopkins in Burlington, Vermont. Upon return to Boston enters the Boston Latin School.

1837   Enters Harvard with the class of 1841. Jones Very is his tutor during his freshman year.

1838   Drops out of Harvard for one year because of trouble with his eyes.

1839   Enters Dean Law College at Harvard with the class of 1842.

1842   Graduates from law school, LL.B. Begins apprenticeship reading law in the Boston office of Edward D. Sohier.

1844   Admitted to the Suffolk County bar. Receives letter of recommendation from Edward D. Sohier. Abandons practice of law.

1847   Purchases home in Greenfield, Massachusetts, from his future father-in-law, David S. Jones, in February. Marries Hannah Lucinda Jones of Greenfield. Begins journal of astronomical observations.

1848   Birth of first son Edward on June 29.

1849   "November" published in *Literary World* (New York) in November.

1850   "April" published in *Literary World* in April.

1851   Travels through England and Scotland. "Hymn: Written upon the Dedication of the Green River Cemetery" (later retitled "Hymn for the Dedication of a Cemetery") read at the dedication on October 7.

1852   "Inspiration," "Infatuation," and "Sonnet" ("Again, again ye part in stormy grief") published in *Living Age* in May.

1853   Birth of daughter Hannah on March 29.

1854   Brother Edward comes to teach at Amherst College, eighteen miles from Greenfield. Tuckerman travels through Europe with wife, Hannah. "Picomegan" published in *Putnam's Monthly Magazine* in July.

1855   Stays with Alfred Lord Tennyson at his house on the Isle of Wight. Tennyson gives him the original manuscript of "Locksley Hall." Correspondence with Tennyson.

1857   Birth of son Frederick on May 7. Death of wife less than a week later.

1860   *Poems* privately printed by John Wilson and Son in Boston. Wilson, the author of *A Treatise on English Punctuation,* is responsible for the punctuation of *Poems*. Wilson produces a unique printer's proof (The Houghton Library "Imperfect Copy"), representing an intermediate stage between the text of the printer's fair copy and that of the corrected, published edition.

1860–1861   Correspondence with Tennyson, Longfellow, Very, Emerson, Hawthorne, William Cullen Bryant, Charles Frederick Briggs, George Ripley, George S. Hillard, James T. Fields, and other literary figures to whom Tuckerman sent copies of *Poems*.

1861   Hopes to publish *Poems* in England, where he imagines the volume would have a better reception. Attempts to interest the English publisher Richard Bentley in taking on trade publication of the book. "Rhotruda" published in *Atlantic Monthly* in July.

1862   "Sonnet" ("The starry flowers, the flower-like stars that fade") published in *Atlantic Monthly* in June, and immediately reprinted in the *Boston Post* and the *Democrat*.

1863   *Poems* published by Smith, Elder and Co. in London, with changes to the edition of 1860. "The starry flower, the flower-like stars that fade" reprinted in the *London Review* in March. "Coralie" and "I took from its glass a flower" published in *Atlantic Monthly* in April. "Picomegan" reprinted in *John Bull* (London). "I took from its glass a flower" reprinted in *Parthenon* (London).

1864   *Poems* published by Ticknor and Fields in Boston, and issued with an errata slip attesting Tuckerman's approval of the text. "Margites" reprinted in *Round Table* (New York) in March.

1867–1868   Corresponds with Hawthorne's widow about the possibility of purchasing Wayside in Concord.

1869   *Poems* published by Little, Brown and Co. in Boston, without an errata slip, and probably without Tuckerman's knowledge. Writes "The Shore."

1870   Writes "Ode. for the Greenfield Soldiers Monument" at the request of the citizens of Greenfield, for the dedication ceremony on October 6.

1870–1871   Moves into a boarding residence, the American House, in Greenfield.

1871   Death of son Edward.

1873   Records fair copies of unpublished poems in a notebook, including a finished version of "The Cricket," the exact text of which is printed in this edition. Sends "An Incident" to the *Springfield Republican* (where it does not appear) on February 7. Dies of heart disease in Greenfield on May 9.

SELECTED POEMS OF FREDERICK

GODDARD TUCKERMAN

November.

OH! who is there of us that has not felt
The sad decadence of the failing year,
And marked the lesson still with grief and fear
Writ in the rollèd leaf, and widely dealt?
When now no longer burns yon woodland belt   5
Bright with disease; no tree in glowing death
Leans forth a cheek of flame to fade and melt
In the warm current of the west wind's breath;
Nor yet through low blue mist, on slope and plain,
Droops the red sunlight in a dream of day;   10
But, from that lull, the winds of change have burst
And dashed the drowsy leaf with shattering rain,
And swung the groves, and roared, and wreaked their worst,
Till all the world is harsh, and cold, and gray.

April.

THE first of April! yet November's haze
Hangs on the wood, and blurs the hill's blue tip:
The light of noon rests wanly on the strip
Of sandy road; recalling leaf-laid ways,
Shades stilled in death, and tender twilight days   5
Ere Winter lifts the wind-trump to his lip.
No moss is shyly seen a tuft to raise,
Nor under grass a gold-eyed flower to dip;
Nor sound is breathed, but haply the south-west
Faint rippling in the brushes of the pine,   10
Or of the shrunken leaf, dry-fluttering.
Compact the village lies, a whitened line
Gathered in smoke. What holds this brooding rest?
Is it dead Autumn? or the dreaming Spring?

May Flowers.

WHERE the dwarf pine reddens
The rocks and soil with its rusted leaves
    And skeleton cones;
    And the footstep deadens,
As it clambers o'er roots and broken stones;   5
While a noise of waves the ear deceives
As the sigh of the wind through the foliage heaves,
    And the restless heart saddens
    With the surging tones;
      Where falls no change   10
From the best and brightest of spring-tide hours,
And the children of Summer their gifts estrange,
    When dashing with flowers
Lowland, and upland, and craggy range:—
There, where Decay and chilled Life stared together   15
    Forlornly round;

In an April day of wilful weather,
The hidden Spring I found.

———

Ere the Month, in bays and hollows,
   Strung with leaves the alder spray,   20
Or with bloom, on river-shallows,
   Dropped the wands of willows gray;

Ere her fingers flung the cowslip
   Golden through the meadow-glade,
Or the bloodroot's caps of silver   25
   Flickered where her feet had played;

Whilst above the bluffs were hiding
   Sullen brows in slouching snows,—
Through the leaves my footstep sliding
   Fell where hers first touched and rose.   30

Underneath the dead pine-droppings,
   Breaking white through mildewed mould,
Gleamed a rosy chain of flowerets,—
   Rosy flowerets, fresh and cold:

Swept not, but by shadow swaying   35
   Of wild branch in windy air,
Couched the buds, unguessed, and laying
   Star to star, in darkness there.

Eagerly, yet half reluctant,
   As the daylight lit on them,   40
Of its clinging tufts of odour
   Quick I stript the trailing stem;

And their lights in cluster blending,—
   Barren sounds and damp decays

Sank, in sighs of Summer ending   45
   And a smell of balmy days.

So refreshed and fancy-solaced,
   Through the Shadow on I past;
While Life seemed to beat and kindle
   In the breath my darlings cast.   50

As I parted from the pine-trees,
   Gathering in, as round a grave
Mourners close;—above their branches,
   From a glimmering western cave,

Sunlight broke into the valley;   55
   Filling with an instant glow
All its basin, from the brook-bed
   To the dark edge touched with snow:

And, by luring sweet, and lustre,
   Summoned from his rock or tree,   60
Heavily, round leaf and cluster,
   Hurtled the bewildered bee.

So, until I found the village,
   Welcome brightened in the air,—
Where, from porch and vine-filled window,   65
   Beamed a welcome still more fair,—

Girlish heads, half-seen, and glancing,
   Peeped athrough the leaf-lorn bowers;
And the little children, dancing,
   Clapped their hands, and cried "May flowers!"   70

* * * * * * * *

Since I found that buried garland,
   Fair, and fresh, and rosy-cold,

All has been its life foreshadowed,—
    Woods in umbrage banked and rolled,

Meadows brimmed with clover, ridges   75
    Where through fern the lupine crowds,
And upon the sandstone ledges
    Laurel heaped like sunset clouds:

But the wayward mind, regretful,
    Wanders through that April day,   80
And, by fields for ever faded,
    Seems to tread a vanished way,

Till it finds those low lights flushing
    Through the pine-trees' mouldered spines,
And hears still the mournful gushing   85
    Of the north wind in the pines.

Hymn for the Dedication of a Cemetery.

BESIDE the River's dark green flow—
    Here, where the pine-trees weep,
Red Autumn's winds will coldly blow
    Above their dreamless sleep;

Their sleep, for whom with prayerful breath   5
    We've put apart to-day,
This spot,—for shadowed walks of Death,
    And gardens of Decay.

This crumbling bank with Autumn crowned,
    These pining woodland ways,   10
Seem now no longer common ground;
    But each in turn conveys

A saddened sense of something more:
    Is it the dying year?

Or a dim shadow, sent before,   15
   Of the next gathering here?

Is it that He, the silent Power,
   Has now assumed the place,
And drunk the light of Morning's hour,
   The life of Nature's grace?   20

Not so: the spot is beautiful,
   And holy is the sod;
'Tis we are faint, our eyes are dull;
   All else is fair in God.

So let them lie, their graves bedecked,   25
   Whose bones these shades invest,
Nor grief deny, nor fear suspect,
   The beauty of their rest.

Infatuation.

'TIS his one hope: all else that round his life
So fairly circles, scarce he numbers now.
The pride of name, a lot with blessings rife,
Determined friends, great gifts that him endow,
Are shrunk to nothing in a woman's smile: 5
Counsel, reproof, entreaty, all are lost,
Like windy waters which their strength exhaust,
And leave no impress; worldly lips revile
With sneer and stinging gibe; but idly by,
Unfelt, unheard, the impatient arrows fly.   10
Careless, he joins a parasitic train,—
Fops, fools, and flatterers, whom her arts enchain,
Nor counts aught base that may to her pertain.
Immersed in love, or what he deems is such,
The present exigence he looks to please,   15
Nor seeks beyond; but only strives to clutch

That which will goad his heart, but ne'er can ease:
So the drenched sailor, wrecked in Indian seas,
To some low reef of wounding coral clings
Mid slav'ry weed, and drift, and ocean scurf;   20
Yet heedeth not companionship of these,
But strains his quivering grasp, and stoutly swings,
Despite of lifting swell and flinging surf.

Sonnet.

AGAIN, again, ye part in stormy grief
From these bare hills, and bowers so built in vain,
And lips and hearts that will not move again,—
Pathetic Autumn, and the writhled leaf;
Dropping away in tears with warning brief: 5
The wind reiterates a wailful strain,
And on the skylight beats the restless rain,
And vapour drowns the mountain, base and brow.
I watch the wet black roofs through mist defined,
I watch the raindrops strung along the blind,   10
And my heart bleeds, and all my senses bow
In grief; as one mild face, with suffering lined,
Comes up in thought: oh wildly, rain and wind,
Mourn on! she sleeps, nor heeds your angry sorrow now.

Picomegan.

STARS of gold the green sod fretting,
Clematis the thicket netting,
Silvery moss her locks down-letting
    Like a maiden brave:
Arrowhead his dark flag wetting   5
    In thy darker wave.

By the River's broken border
    Wading through the ferns,
When a darker deep, and broader,
    Fills its bays and turns;   10
Up along the winding ridges,
    Down the sudden-dropped descent,
Rounding pools with reedy edges,
    Silent coves in alders pent,—
Through the river-flags and sedges   15
    Dreamily I went.

Dreamily, for perfect Summer
   Hushed the vales with misty heat;
In the wood, a drowsy drummer,
   The woodpecker, faintly beat;   20
Songs were silent, save the voices
   Of the mountain and the flood,
Save the wisdom of the voices
   Only known in solitude:
But to me, a lonely liver,   25
   All that fading afternoon
From the undermining river
   Came a burden in its tune;—
Came a tone my ear remembers,
   And I said, "What grief thee grieves,   30
Pacing through thy leafy chambers,
   And thy voice of rest bereaves?
Winds of change that wail and bluster,
   Sunless morns, and shivering eves,
Carry sweets to thee belonging,—   35
   All of light thy rim receives;
River-growths that fold and cluster,
   Following where the waters lead,
Bunches of the purple aster,
   Mints, and blood-dropped jewel-weed,   40
Like carnelians hanging
   'Mid their pale-green leaves:
Wherefore then, with sunlight heaping
   Perfect joy and promised good,
When thy flow should pulse in keeping   45
   With the beating of the blood,
Through thy dim green shadows sweeping,
When the folded heart is sleeping,
   Dost thou mourn and brood?"

Wider, wilder, round the headland,   50
    Black the River swung,
Over skirt and hanging woodland
    Deeper stillness hung,
As once more I stood a dreamer
    The waste weeds among.   55
Doubt, and pain, and grief extremer,
    Seemed to fall away:
But a dim voluptuous sorrow
Smote and thrilled my fancy thoro',
    Gazing over bend and bay;   60
Saying, "Thou, O mournful River!
    As of old dost wind and waste;
Falling down the reef for ever,
    Rustling with a sound of haste
Through the dry-fringed meadow-bottom;   65
    But my hands, aside thy bed,
Gather now no gems of Autumn,
    Or the dainties Summer shed:
By the margin hoarsely flowing,
Yellow-dock and garget growing,   70
Drifts of wreck, and muddy stain,
By river-wash, and dregs of rain.
Yet, though bound in desolation,
    Bound and locked, thy waters pour,
With a cry of exultation   75
    Uncontained by shore and shore;
With a booming, deep vibration,
    In its wind my cheek is wet,—
But, unheeding woe or warning,
    Thou through all the barren hours   80
    Seem'st to sing of Summer yet;
Thou, with voice all sorrow scorning,

Babblest on of leaves and flowers
Wearily, whilst I go mourning
   O'er thy fallen banks and bowers; 85
O'er a life small grace adorning,
   With lost aims, and broken powers
Wreck-flung, like these wave-torn beaches,
   Tear-trenched, as by winter showers.
But a faith thy music teaches, 90
   Might I to its knowledge climb,
Still the yearning heart beseeches
   Truth; as when in summer time
Through these dells I vaguely sought her,
   In the dreamy summer time." 95
So the margin paths and reaches
   Once again I left to roam,
Left behind the roaring water,
   Eddy-knots, and clots of foam;
But it still disturbed me ever, 100
   As a dream no reason yields,
From the ruin of the river,
   Winding up through empty fields,
That I could not gather something
   Of the meaning and belief, 105
In the voice of its triumphing,
   Or the wisdom of its grief.

Sonnets.

I.

THE starry flower, the flower-like stars that fade
And brighten with the daylight and the dark,—
The bluet in the green I faintly mark,
And glimmering crags with laurel overlaid,
Even to the Lord of light, the Lamp of shade,   5
Shine one to me,—the least, still glorious made
As crownèd moon, or heaven's great hierarch.
And, so, dim grassy flower, and night-lit spark,
Still move me on and upward for the True;
Seeking through change, growth, death, in new and old.   10
The full in few, the statelier in the less,
With patient pain; always remembering this,—
His hand, who touched the sod with showers of gold,
Stippled Orion on the midnight blue.

II.

AND so, as this great sphere (now turning slow   15
Up to the light from that abyss of stars,
Now wheeling into gloom through sunset bars)—
With all its elements of form and flow,
And life in life; where crowned, yet blind, must go
The sensible king,—is but a Unity   20
Compressed of motes impossible to know;
Which worldlike yet in deep analogy,
Have distance, march, dimension, and degree;
So the round earth—which we the world do call—
Is but a grain in that that mightiest swells,   25
Whereof the stars of light are particles,
As ultimate atoms of one infinite Ball,
On which God moves, and treads beneath his feet the All!

Twilight.

1.

IN the darkening silence,—
When the hilltops dusk and fail,
And the purple damps of evening now
No longer edge the vale;
When the faint flesh-tinted clouds have parted   5
To the westward, one by one,—
In the glimmering silence,
I love to steal alone
By river and by runside,
Through knots of aspens gray,   10
And hearken for the voices
Of a music ceased away.

2.

    About the winding water,
    And among the bulrush-spears,
  Like the wind of empty Autumn, comes   15
      Their sorrow in my ears;
Like the wind of hollow Autumn blowing
    From swamp and shallow dim,
    Comes the sorrow of the voices;
    Whilst along the weedy brim   20
    I follow in the evenfall,
    And darkly reason why
    Those whispers breathe so mournfully
    From depths of days gone by.

3.

    Is it that, in the stealing   25
    Of the tender, tearful tones,
  The knowledge stirs, that bowers and homes
    Are dust and fallen stones,
Where once they sang?—that on lips so loving
    Settled a still gray sleep,   30
    With tears, though mindful memory
    Still brings them from the deep?
    Is it that Conscience muses,
    "'Twas for thee their high hearts heaved?"
    Or is it so, that I am not   35
    What those best hearts believed?

4.

    O falling stream! O voices!
    O grief! O gaining night!
  Ye bring no comfort to the heart:
    Ye but again unite   40
In a brooding gloom, and a windy wail;
    And a sorrow, cold like Death,
    Steals from the river-border,
    Falls in the dampening breath
    Of the unavailing night-wind,—   45
    Falls with the strength of tears,
    And an unreal bitterness,
    On the life of latter years.

5.

    I see the flags of the River,
    And the moss-green alder bark,   50
  While faintly the far-set village lights
    Flash through the rainy dark;
And the willow drops to the dipping water,—
    But why, from shelf and shore,
    Comes the trouble of the voices   55
    Of the loved of heretofore?
    They never knew these shadows,
    And the river's sighing flow
    Swept not their ears in those dim days,
    Nor lulled them long ago.   60

6.

Sunk are the ships, or shattered,—
Yet, as 'mid the burying foam,
On the wild sea-bar, beat here and there,
As the surges go and come,
Pieces and parts of a broken vessel;   65
So, to this stranger stream
And its still woods, come drifting in,
Thought, memory, doubt, and dream,
Of the noble hearts that sailed with me:
Here to this desert spot   70
Come their dim ghosts, where they, indeed,
Were known and nurtured not.

7.

'Tis the heart, the heart, remembers,
And with wild and passionate will
Peoples the woods and vales, and pours   75
Its cry round stream and hill.
I look o'er the hills to the mournful morning,
And it whispers still of home,—
And, in the darkening of the day,
Impels me forth to roam,   80
With a desolate and vague desire,
Like the evil spirit's quest;
Who walketh through dry places,
Seeking still, nor finding rest.

8.

     Yet, in the gathering silence,   85
     When the hilltops faint and fail,
  And the tearful tints of twilight now
     No longer edge the vale;
When the crimson-faded clouds have parted
     To the westward, one by one,—   90
     In the passionate silence,
     I love to steal alone
     By river and by runside,
     Through knots of aspens gray,
     And hearken for the voices   95
     Of a music ceased away.

To the River.

'Tis nearly night,—a healing night,
    As Carro's words last-spoken,
"And will the day be blue and bright?
    A whole bright day, unbroken?"
You ask of me, who walk to learn;   5
    Regardless wealth amassing,
And take no charge of tide or turn,
    And scarcely keep, in passing,

A watch on wind and weather-gleam,—
    Of these things no recorder;   10
Yet o'er the dark I almost seem
    To see its golden border.
Behind the night is hid the day:
    I cannot find the reason
In rule or rhyme; but all things say   15
    'Twill be a day of season.

And Carro, too, will softer smile,
    And Carro's frown be rarer,
But leave your fair a little while,—
    You'll find her all the fairer,—   20
To walk with me; not by the road,
    (A little breathing give her,)
And we will keep the winding wood
    Until we strike the River.

And I will tell, where Love, though loath,   25
    A fuller harvest heapeth
Than yours: yet I have known the growth,
    And followed where he reapeth;
And this, though now to heaven you cast,
    Appealing, death-defiant,   30
A passion pitiless and vast
    As love of god or giant!

For one is beat with blasting tears,
    And burned with raging weather,
And reapt in fiery haste,—the ears   35
    Half-ripe, dead-ripe, or neither:
The other hangs with dim rain prest,
    All greenly wet, and groweth
For ever in the realms of rest,
    Nor end nor seedtime knoweth.   40

Yet some, who cannot help to see,
    Refuse the day, and many,
Where faintest strokes of sunlight be,
    Peep hard for pin and penny,
Who sneer at what the meadow spreads,   45
    And what the woods environ;
And, like the sons of Use, with heads,
    And hands, and feet of iron,

Would grasp the Titan's scythe to wound;
    To sweep the hill asunder,   50
And shear the groves at one swing-round,
    And tread the Muses under!
Yet, still best-pleased amid the roar,
    I find myself a debtor,
Love men not lesser than before,   55
    And Nature more than better.

There be, with brains no folding shroud
    Of grief, can wean or widow
Of vacant mirth, who bear the cloud,
    Yet shrink from shade of shadow;   60
Would flit for ever in the shine,
    Despite of burns and blisters,
And add another to the Nine,
    More foolish than her sisters:

A denary of graceful girls,   65
    That carol, dance, and sidle
Through chaffering crowds, and giddying whirls
    Of Life, all loud and idle.
But I, who love the graver Muse,
    And Minna more than Brenda,   70
Walk not with these, nor find my views
    Writ down in their credenda.

Why, for some peep of meaning clear,
    Should we ourselves deliver
Up to the stream, which even here   75
    Roars past us like a River?
But bend, and let the hurly pass,—
    Pedant and fop, chance-hitters!
Whilst, in the fields of faded grass,
    The cricket ticks and twitters;—   80

With those that loose the languid page,
    Nor let the life o'erflow it,
But pick and copy, sap and sage:
    Part wit, and parcel poet,
They follow fast some empiric,   85
    Nor heed for watch or warden;
But go in crowds, and settle thick
    Like crows in Nature's garden.

They chew the sweet, and suck the sour,
    And know not which is sweeter,—   90
The cowslip, and calypso flower,
    Bald breath, and burning metre,
Milton, or Skelton,—all is one;
    None darkle dim where none shine:
And with a blindness of their own   95
    They blot the breeze and sunshine.

Oh, might I plunge beneath the flow
    For one forgetful minute,
And, leaving all my dreams below,
    Rise like a bubble in it,   100
And sweep along to lose myself
    With all the current seizes;
But in the blows of brass and delf
    I fear to go to pieces!

Perhaps my hand would urge the cup   105
    To press apart a nation,
Or, where the Fountain forces up,
    Drop tears of congelation;
Or pull with them that strain to drag
    The chords of Union tauter,   110
Stream to the polls with club and flag,
    And crossed with sacred water.

But hold! nor cloud our night with these:
    Why should we crowd or quarrel?
Look! in the west the Golden Bees   115
    Hang o'er the mountain laurel;
And, see! in every spot of wet,
    The coltsfoot groups and glistens;
While, with a dew,—the holiest yet,—
    Young Night her children christens.   120

Why should *I* set my feeble strength
    A bitter blame to cancel,
Or hold a traitor up at length,
    Or tear away a tinsel,
Or beat about for bribe or boon;   125
    When here, in pool and shallow,
I see the fragment of a moon,
    Rimmed with a fragment halo?

A Soul that out of Nature's Deep.

I.
A SOUL that out of Nature's deep
    From inner fires had birth;
Yet not as rocks or rosebuds peep:
    Nor came it to the earth

II.
A drop of rain at random blown;   5
    A star-point burning high,
Lit in the dark, and as alone
    As Lyra in the sky:

III.
Nor ushered in with stormy air,
    Sea-shock, or earthquake-jars;   10
Nor born to fame beneath some rare
    Conspiracy of stars;

IV.

Nor fortune-crowned with benefits:
    The life was larger lent,
Made up of many opposites   15
    In contradiction blent:—

V.

A nature affable and grand,
    Yet cold as headland snow,
Large-handed, liberal to demand,
    Though still to proffer slow;   20

VI.

That shunned to share the roaring cup,
    The toast, and cheerings nine,
Nor cared to sit alone to sup
    The pleasure of the wine;

VII.

Yet genial oft by flash and fit;   25
    High manners, courage mild,—
God gave him these, and savage wit
    As to an Indian child:

VIII.

And gave him more than this indeed,—
    The wisdom to descry   30
A weathercock in the waving weed,
    A clock-face in the sky.

IX.

But he, amid these bowers and dales
   A larger life-breath drew,
Beneath more cordial sunshine, gales,   35
   And skies of sounder blue,

X.

Than wait on all. Beside the brook,
   With far forgetful eye,
Or toward the deep hills, would he look,
   Watching the glory die;   40

XI.

Brooding in dim solicitude
   On earlier, other times,
And yon dark-purple wing of wood
   That o'er the mountain climbs;

XII.

And fancies thick like flower-buds bright;   45
   Rare thoughts in affluence rank,
Came at the onset of the light,
   Nor with the sunset sank.

XIII.

He slept not, but the dream had way,
   And his watch abroad was cast   50
With the earliest light of the earliest day;
   And, when the light fell fast,

XIV.

He stood in the river-solitudes
   To mark the daylight go;
And low in the dusk of the wailing woods   55
   He heard the night-hawk blow.

XV.

The night-hawk, and the whippoorwill
    Across the plashes dim,
Calling her mate from bower and hill,
    Made prophecy for him: 60

XVI.

The night-hawk and the bird bereaved,
    His airy calendars,
He stood; till night had, unperceived,
    Surrounded him with stars.

XVII.

Oh! dear the look of upward eyes   65
    Lifted with pleading might,
A smile to bless and humanize,
    A hand to fold aright;

XVIII.

A silver voice to lead and lull;
    Slight step, and streamy hair,—   70
But, oh! she was too beautiful
    That he should call her fair.

XIX.

A love to pay, a life to give,
    Was hers,—for this she strove;
And he, too, loved, and would not live   75
    To live out of her love.

XX.

And childhood came his smile beneath,
    And lingered hour on hour,
With sweepy lids, and innocent breath
    Like the grape-hyacinth flower.   80

XXI.

For this, for all, his heart was full;
    Yet, to the deeper mind,
All outward passion seemed to dull
    That inmost sense refined

XXII.

That broods and feeds where few have trod;   85
    And seeks to pass apart,
Imaging nature, man, and God,
    In silence in the heart.

XXIII.

He saw—for to that secret eye
    God's hidden things were spread—   90
The wiser world in darkness lie,
    And Faith by Falsehood led.

XXIV.

Virtue and Envy, side by side;
    Blind Will that walks alone;
And mighty throngs that come and glide,   95
    Unknowing and unknown;

XXV.

Great lights! but quenched; strength, foresight, skill,
    Gone without deed or name;
And happy accidents that still
    Misplace the wreaths of fame;   100

XXVI.

Religion, but a bruited word
    'Twixt foes who difference view
Between our Saviour, God the Lord,
    And Jesus Christ the Jew!

XXVII.

Yet unto all, one wall and fold;   105
    One bed that all must share,—
The miser brooding holy gold,
    The fool, and spendthrift heir;

XXVIII.

Still through the years the wrinkled chuff
    Acre to acre rolled;   110
And he, too, will have land enough
    When his mouth is filled with mould.

XXIX.

And vaster visions did he win
    From cloud, and mountain bars,
And revelations that within   115
    Fell like a storm of stars!

XXX.

Yet checked and crossed by doubt and night;
    Dim gulfs, and solitudes
Of the deep mind; or warmth and light
    Broke from its shifting moods,   120

XXXI.

As when in many-weathered March
    May-buds break up through snow,
And, spilt like milk, beneath the larch
    The little bluets blow;

XXXII.

Beneath the lilac and the larch   125
    In many a splash and spot;
Nor belting sea, nor heaven's blue arch,
    Bound in where these were not—

XXXIII.

With Love and Peace: yet strangely sank
    Cold sorrow on his soul,   130
For human wisdom, and the blank
    Summation of the whole.

XXXIV.

Nor seemed it fit, that one, unnerved
    And faint, should rouse the earth;
Or build with those whose zeal had served   135
    But to incense his mirth.

XXXV.

Troubled to tears, he stood and gazed,—
    Unknowing where to weep,
To spend his cries o'er fabrics razed,
    Or a safe silence keep;   140

XXXVI.

Renouncing human life and lore;
    Love's calm, and love's excess,
Experience and allegiance, for
    A higher passiveness.

XXXVII.

So to drink full of Nature, much   145
    Recipient, still to woo
Her windy walk, where pine-trees touch
    Against the ribby blue;

XXXVIII.

To find her feet by singing rills,
    Adoring and alone,—   150
O'er grassy fields, to the still hills,
    Her solemn seat and throne!

XXXIX.

Sore struggle! yet, when passed, that seemed
    A crowning conquest o'er
Himself and human bands: he deemed   155
    The victory more and more,

XL.

And like that warfare urged upon
    Unkingly lust and ease,
Which the fifth Henry waged and won;
    Or that Lydiades   160

XLI.

Who left his looser life with tears,
    And in the fire of youth
Lived grave and chaste, Arcadian years
    And reigned;—kings, heroes, both!

XLII.

Ah, so—but not to him returned,   165
    Our monarch, meed like this,
But sterner kin his grief had spurned,
    And bitter friends were his.

XLIII.

Distrust and Fear beside him took,
    With Shame, their hateful stands;   170
And Sorrow passed, and struck the book
    Of knowledge from his hands.

XLIV.

He saw, with absent, sorrowing heed,
    All that had looked so fair;
His secret walk was wild with weed,   175
    His gardens washed and bare:

XLV.

The very woods were filled with strife;
　　Fierce beaks and warring wings
Clashed in his face; the heart and life
　　Of those deep-hidden springs,　　　　　　　　　180

XLVI.

No more his spirit cared to quaff:
　　Great Nature lost her place,—
Pushed from her happy heights, and half
　　Degraded of her grace.

XLVII.

And so he saw the morning white,　　　　　　　　185
　　As eyes with tears opprest,
The last heart-breaking gleam of light
　　That dies along the West.

XLVIII.

And so he saw the opening flower
　　Dry in the August sheaf,　　　　　　　　　　190
And on green Summer's top and tower,
　　Only the turning leaf:

XLIX.

For Summer's darkest green, explored,
　　Betrays the crimson blight;
As, in the heart of darkness cored,　　　　　　　195
　　Red sparks and seeds of light

L.

And lightning lurk, ready to leap
　　Abroad, beyond reclaim;
To bathe a world in splendour deep,
　　Or snatch in folding flame.　　　　　　　　　200

LI.

He saw, with manners, age, and mode,
   Opinion rise and sink,
The jarring clash of creed and code,
   And knew not what to think;—

LII.

Beliefs of ritual and of race;—   205
   And hard it was to tell
Why good should come by gift of grace,
   And wrong be chargeable.

LIII.

Before him burned attainless towers!
   Behind, a comfortless   210
Dim valley, waste with poison-flowers,
   And weeds of barrenness.

LIV.

The early ray, the early dream,
   Had vanished; faint and chill
Like winter, did the morning stream   215
   On woodland, house, and hill:

LV.

Yet, as of old, he ranged apart
   By river-bank and bed,
And mused in bitterness of heart;
   And to himself he said,—   220

LVI.

"Tear sullen Monkshood where he stands
   Tall by the garden walk;
With burning pricks and venom-glands,
   Pluck off the nettle's stalk;

LVII.

Lobelia from the rivage break,   225
    With Arum's blistering bell;
And, over all, let the bundle reek
    With the smilax' loathly smell;

LVIII.

Fools' parsley from the graves of fools,
    With deadly darnels bring;   230
Yew, garget, dogwood of the pools,
    And the fen's unwholesome spring;

LIX.

And hemlock pull; and snatch from bees
    Half-drugged, the red-bud rare,
And laurel; but prick in with these   235
    The shaft of a lily fair;

LX.

And bind them up; rank blossom, sting,
    Bough, berry, poison rife,
Embodying and embleming
    The gleanings of a life."   240

LXI.

Yet was not she, the lily-flower,
    'Mid failings and misdeeds,
The fruit of many a scattered hour,
    Yet fairer for the weeds?

LXII.

And was she not, through shade and shower,   245
    In patient beauty drest,
Though lonely in her place and power,
    Enough to save the rest?

LXIII.

Perhaps; yet darker gloomed the vale,
    And dawned the turrets fair,   250
Beyond the height of ladder's scale,
    Or any step of stair.

LXIV.

And yearned his soul for sharper change,—
    And knowledge of the light;
Yet not by station, staff, or range   255
    Of human toil or flight,

LXV.

Would he ascend; choosing alone
    With grief to make his bed,
Like those whose godhead is their own;
    On whom the curse is said,—   260

LXVI.

Who kindle to themselves a fire,
    And in the light thereof
Walk, and are lost. But his desire
    Was still for wiser love;

LXVII.

And sought but in the holy place;   265
    And scarcely sought, but found
In still reception: failing this,
    All life in death seemed drowned.

LXVIII.

Yet sometimes, doubting, discord-tost,
    Came voices to his side,—   270
Echoes of youth, and friendships lost,
    Or lost, or left aside.

LXIX.

Faces, wherein deep histories are,
  Began to float and flee,
And hover darkly, like a far   275
  Forgotten memory;

LXX.

Dim gardens, where a silent creek
  Stole onward, margin-mossed;
And walks, with here and there a streak
  Of dusky odour crossed,   280

LXXI.

Stirring the wells of tears. He saw
  The vision of his youth,
With holy grief, with holy awe:
  The temple-towers of Truth

LXXII.

Broke nearer; like a thunder-flash   285
  Again came back the dream,
And light in many a bar and dash,
  Like moonlight, flake, and beam,

LXXIII.

Or when wild clouds of middle air
  Through hurrying gaps reveal   290
Arcturus, or the sailing star
  That spurs Orion's heel;—

LXXIV.

Heaven's lights! yet covered as we look;
  So, momently to view,
Came back the sparkle of the brook,   295
  And fields his childhood knew;

LXXV.

Fair faith and love, with peace almost;
    Yet, in that ray serene,
He only saw a glory lost,
    And what he might have been.   300

LXXVI.

The precious grains his hands had spilled
    Had fallen to others; they
Had passed before, his place was filled,
    And the world rolled away.

LXXVII.

Too late he learned that Nature's parts   305
    Whereto we lean and cling,
Change, but as change our human hearts,
    Nor grow by worshipping;

LXXVIII.

And that her presence, fair or grand,
    In these faint fields below,   310
Importeth little, seen beyond
    Our welfare, or our woe.

LXXIX.

Nor good from ill can we release,—
    But weigh the world in full;
Not separate taken, part and piece,   315
    But indiscerptible.

LXXX.

In law and limit, tempests blow;
    Tides swing from shore to shore;
And so the forest-tree will grow
    As grew the tree before.   320

LXXXI.

Too late he learned by land and sea
  This bitter truth to glean,—
That he who would know what shall be,
  Must ponder what hath been;

LXXXII.

Nor unto fear or falsehood yield   325
  His strength, the good to baulk;
Nor fold his arms beside the field,
  But *with* the furrow walk,

LXXXIII.

Ready to cast his grain; and slower
  To faint, more credulous,   330
Believing well that but by our
  Own hands God helpeth us.

LXXXIV.

And who would find out Wisdom's grot,
  To make her footsteps his,—
Must learn to look where it is not,   335
  As well as where it is.

A Sample of Coffee Beans,
SENT TO THE AUTHOR, WITH A REQUEST FOR A POEM;
OR,
THE PUBLICAN, THE PEDDLER, AND THE POET.

TWELVE plain brown beans! 'Twould seem to ask
   As plain, indeed, a string of verses:
But beans are sweet; and though my task
   Must deal with these, and, what far worse is,
A story dry must dress or dock,   5
   So to search out fair Truth, or shun her,—
Yet may I garnish up the stock,
   And hang it with the scarlet runner.

The bean, the garden-bean, I sing,—
   Lima, mazagan, late and early,   10
Bush, butter, black eye, pole and string,
   Esculent, annual, planted yearly:
Sure here a poet well might fare,
   Nor vaguely his invention worry;
I shake my head in flat despair;   15
   Or out and over the hills I hurry,

As Io fled by Nigris' stream,—
    Spurred by the angry brize or bot-bee:
But beans I sing, a classic theme
    Known to the Muse; and may they not be   20
Melodious made in other than
    The lyric verse or amœbæan,—
Beans, hateful to the banished man,
    And banned by the Pythagorean?

Loose, or in legume blue and red,   25
    Tinged like a tom-turkey's wattle;
Or strung like birds' eggs on a thread;
    Or stiff and dry in pods they rattle:
Beans too, in bladders, discomposed
    By stroke and blow, make music mystic;   30
But these are free in hand, nor closed
    In their own natural cells, or cystic.

May I not, inly pondering, see,
    Or stumbling on in flight phrenetic,
Enough of truth and simile,   35
    To strew the way with flowers poetic?
No! though on every side they fell,
    Dispersed like the gold hemony
On Ulai's bank, with asphodel,
    Lote, lily-blow, and anemone,   40

Beans would be beans, the gardener's joy;
    And, though to him more dear than roses,
Not to be made to senses coy
    Rose-redolent, by any process.
Let me, then, cease to stir my breast,   45
    No longer stay to bribe or flatter
The vegetable text; but rest,
    Or get at once into my matter.

A little public-house and bar,
    Barn, corn-house, dovecote, gathered under   50
A mighty elm, which, arching far,
    Held off the rain and drew the thunder;
A farmstead small of shabby huts,
    Unknown to cane or cotton grower,
And just within the line that cuts   55
    The States, and Canada the Lower:

A little public-house and bar
    Smelling of beer and dead tobacco,
It stood; within, a bench and chair,
    A parrot, and an ape; but Jacko   60
Was stuffed above the chimney-piece,
    And Poll was plaster: so we summon
The holders of our house of ease,
    And live incumbents, man and woman.

Jolly and old the landlord was,   65
    Part farmer, and part broadcloth-smuggler;
The wife a patient drudge, alas!
    With aches and asthma long a struggler;
Yet day and night she served the grate:
    He scarcely past beyond the groundsill;   70
But, feet in slipper-shoes, sat late,
    And drew his ale, and kept his counsel.

Above his head an almanac
    Depended, while the slate and pencil,
On toddy-stick and tumbler-rack,   75
    Kept watch, and stood to charge or cancel:
Nought else, except a faded, grim,
    Fly-spattered print of Buonaparté,
And the host's Sunday hat and trim,
    Hung, like their owner, plump and hearty.   80

Another too, a poet slim,
    Came nightly from the neighbour-village
To this retreat; more sweet to him
    Than leafy summer-house, or treillage
Wherethrough the moonbeams fall: the wreath   85
    Trailed from the pipe of passing drover,
More rare than the grape-blossom's breath,
    Or night-gusts o'er the beds of clover.

In the world-drama he was one,
    Bearing, perhaps, a part like Peto   90
In the old play: yet did he shun
    The world, and, reckless of mosquito,
By pond-hole dark, and weedy drain,
    Sequestered swamp, or grassy side-hill,
Would linger, breathing dull disdain   95
    In many a rustic ode and idyll;

And breathing beauty too, and wit;
    Nor lacked it in poetic ardour,
His verse; for, where he doubted it,
    He struck again, and hammered harder: 100
'Twas hit or miss, to make or maul,—
    Not quite a Walter Scott or Byron,—
Two blows upon the anvil fall,
    And one upon the burning iron!

Good fellow was he in the main,   105
    Yet strangely strove to be unhappy,
Himself a desert-chief would feign,
    And Cow-cliff, Ararat or Api;
Or, all alone, would weep, to cleanse
    Some fancied shame or felony;   110
Or, witchlike, haunt the birchwood glens
    For vervain dank and chélone.

A chamber, too, he had at times
   For needful rest: but his ambition
Was still to read and rant his rhymes,   115
   Unwearied with their repetition;
Or over some old tale bemused
   To lie, till chilled and hunger-bitten,
Along a floor with books confused,
   And blotted sheets, and rolls o'erwritten.   120

Full well he knew the stars and flowers,
   The atmosphere, its height and pressure,
The laws that gird the globe, and powers
   That make our peril or our pleasure.
He knew each bird, its range and sphere;   125
   For plant and shrub, had many an odd use:
But naught of farming-growths or gear,
   And less of garden-sauce and produce:

So when the peddler passed, and brought
   His last new lot of lies and lumber,—   130
Tins, foot-stove, gridiron, pail, and pot,
   And drugs, and dry-goods, without number;
Cigars too in the grocery line;
   Tracts, extracts, jellies, quince, or guava,
And, rarest, seed for coffee-vine,   135
   Pure bean or berry, just from Java;

He listened: "Sure to sprout; in fall
   To ripen, let the world go onward,
A row of oaken scrags was all
   They needed, so to scramble sunward."   140
"O happy thou," the schoolslip read,
   "Who with thy hands thy fortune carvest!"
"But happiest," so the peddler said,
   "Is he who gets such grain in harvest."

And so they talked. The summer wind   145
   Came softly from the meadow blowing,
Through open door and window-blind
   Brought the pine's breath across the mowing;
It stirred the print, it jarred the slate,
   It waved the farmer's best apparel,   150
And shook the dry weeds in the grate,
   And withered grasses, awn and aril.

And still they talked; and, ere the wind
   Had faded, all that parcel precious
Was to our hero's hand resigned   155
   For future use. May such refresh us,
And him who held his luck revealed!
   His own, no doubtful risk or far gain,
But silver planted, sure to yield,
   And bless him with a golden bargain.   160

And then the landlord drew his best;
   No hoarded drops of vintage fruity,
But good to speed the parting guest
   And cheer the new: so while in duty
The poet drank, and called for more,   165
   The landlord, like a desert sandy,
The peddler parted, richer for
   Six dollars and a slug of brandy.

What more? Why, naught. 'Twere slow to tell
   The sequel here; such Glaucian traffic   170
May well befit a Homer's shell,
   Or Virgil's harp; or, sung in Sapphic,
Perhaps 'twould mount a theme divine;
   But, in this mess of jar and jingle,
'Twould pose the nine brains of the Nine   175
   To make much sense and music mingle.

Yet might I tell how hard he wrought,
   Rising betimes to watch his purchase;
And left his rhymes and dreams forgot,
   And lonely walks beneath the birches;   180
And how the vines got riper fast;
   Till, battered pan with sauce-pan clinking,
He borrowed fire, and saw at last
   His prize, burnt, ground, and hot for drinking;

And how the Poet stirred and supt   185
   With an old spoon new-bought at auction,
And thought the world's ways all corrupt,—
   For so he found his pure decoction;
Not fragrant, black, and fit indeed
   To set before a King or Sophi;   190
But slate-stones for his silver seed!
   And, for his coffee-bean, bean-coffee!

His letter, too,—'tis here, addressed
   To some society Botanic,
In languid ink; though fitted best   195
   On wharf and mart to scatter panic.
A massive missive certainly,
   Nor writ with rifled plume of seraph;
See here! the dotless j and i
   Deform, with sprawly date, and paraph.   200

And last, not least, could I repeat
   The landlord's glee, when, thither poking,
The poet sneaked into his seat,
   And all the glory of the joking;
How the old fellow roared, forsooth,   205
   And laughed from shining poll to shoelap;
Whilst the old lady showed her tooth,
   And coughed, and shook the double dewlap.

Enough! the house still stands the same,
　　With barn and steadings; but the elm-tree   210
Went down in a great blow that came
　　To flatten fence and overwhelm tree.
Yet looks the ale-bench on the way,
　　And, as of old, the twain divide it;
But, since the coffee-trade, they say   215
　　The peddler has not passed beside it.

Anybody's Critic.

KEEN, brilliant, shallow, with a ready phrase
To fit occasion, and a happy knack
Of adaptation, where he most did lack,
And witty too, and wise in several ways;
As knowing where to choose, and where to skip: 5
"Passwords of inspiration" on his lip,
He takes the wall; and now may well surprise
Those who remember him five lustrums back,—
A ferret-headed boy with purry eyes.
Behold the Scholar now, the Judge profound!   10
Yet, feeling with his foot precarious ground,
He stands to fly, or, with a borrowed jest,
To blink the question when too closely pressed.
Reproof in praise, and friendship in his frown,
Have we not seen him, talking calmly down   15
On some proud spirit; letting light illapse

On him, poor votary of the book and pen,
Every-ways his superior; perhaps
A mighty Poet, before common men
Ashamed? But view our Critic! mark his eye   20
Exhaustive, nose would snuff the violet dry
Of odour, and a brow to whelm the world.
In his right hand a written leaf is twirled;
Before, a landscape spreads; and there you see,
Skirting the sky, low scrub and topping tree.   25
Beside him stands a youth with bended eyes,
(Waiting the word until the Master rise,)
With blushing brow, less confident than cowed:
Perhaps his poem in his hand he brought;
Or a late letter from some lord of thought,   30
Like a rich gem, half-grudgingly he shows;
Of which a young man might full well be proud;
So cordial, sweet, and friendly to the close,
With not one vacant word of cant or chaff.
"Yes, yes," the Master says, "an autograph!   35
And surely to be prized; for such things *sell:*
And, for your poem, 'tis a clever thing."
Then turning the poor pages carelessly,
As taking in the whole with half an eye,
He said, "The worth of such 'tis hard to tell: 40
If Art inspire us, 'tis in vain we sing;
If love of Nature merely, 'tis not well;
And personal themes have little good or harm:
For in these bustling days, when critics swarm,
No man can stand aside, without rebuke,   45
To prate of bubbling brooks, and uplands grassy;
Like the Pied Piper in the Burgelostrassé,
'Twill set the rats a-running." Then with a look,
A look that took the beauty from the grass,

And damped the blue, he let the subject pass   50
For other themes; glancing at, Heaven knows what!
The farm, the camp, the forum, Pitt and Burke;
And in his confidential, friendly phrase
Weighed that, he knew the other valued not,
Or plainly lacked; and of his life's best work   55
Spoke easily, with depreciating praise.

Rhotruda.

IN the golden reign of Charlemaign the king,
The three and thirtieth year, or thereabout,
Young Eginardus, bred about the court,
(Left mother-naked at a postern-door,)
Had thence by slow degrees ascended up;—   5
First page, then pensioner, lastly the king's knight
And secretary; but held these steps for naught
Save as they led him to the Princess' feet,
Eldest and loveliest of the regal three,
Most gracious too, and liable to love: 10
For Bertha was betrothed; and she, the third,
Giselia, would not look upon a man.
So, bending his whole heart unto this end,
He watched and waited, trusting to stir to fire
The indolent interest in those large eyes,   15

And feel the languid hands beat in his own,
Ere the new spring. And well he played his part;
Slipping no chance to bribe, or brush aside,
All that would stand between him and the light;
Making fast foes in sooth, but feeble friends.   20
But what cared he, who had read of ladies' love,
And how young Launcelot gained his Guenovere;
A foundling too, or of uncertain strain?
And when one morning, coming from the bath,
He crossed the Princess on the palace-stair,   25
And kissed her there in her sweet disarray,
Nor met the death he dreamed of, in her eyes,—
He knew himself a hero of old romance;
Not seconding, but surpassing, what had been.

And so they loved; if that tumultuous pain   30
Be love,—disquietude of deep delight,
And sharpest sadness; nor, though he knew her heart
His very own,—gained on the instant too,
And like a waterfall that at one leap
Plunges from pines to palms,—shattered at once   35
To wreaths of mist, and broken spray bows bright,
He loved not less, nor wearied of her smile;
But through the daytime held aloof and strange
His walk; mingling with knightly mirth and game;
Solicitous but to avoid alone   40
Aught that might make against him in her mind;
Yet strong in this,—that, let the world have end,
He had pledged his own, and held Rhotruda's troth.

But Love, who had led these lovers thus along,
Played them a trick one windy night and cold: 45
For Eginardus, as his wont had been,

Crossing the quadrangle, and under dark,—
No faint moonshine, nor sign of any star,—
Seeking the Princess' door, such welcome found,
The knight forgot his prudence in his love;   50
For lying at her feet, her hands in his,
And telling tales of knightship and emprise,
And ringing war; while up the smooth white arm
His fingers slid insatiable of touch,
The night grew old: still of the hero-deeds   55
That he had seen, he spoke; and bitter blows
Where all the land seemed driven into dust!
Beneath fair Pavia's wall, where Loup beat down
The Longobard, and Charlemaign laid on,
Cleaving horse and rider; then, for dusty drought   60
Of the fierce tale, he drew her lips to his,
And silence locked the lovers fast and long,
Till the great bell crashed One into their dream.

The castle-bell! and Eginard not away!
With tremulous haste she led him to the door,   65
When, lo! the courtyard white with fallen snow,
While clear the night hung over it with stars.
A dozen steps, scarce that, to his own door:
A dozen steps? a gulf impassable!
What to be done? Their secret must not lie   70
Bare to the sneering eye with the first light;
She could not have his footsteps at her door!
Discovery and destruction were at hand:
And, with the thought, they kissed, and kissed again;
When suddenly the lady, bending, drew   75
Her lover towards her half-unwillingly,
And on her shoulders fairly took him there,—

Who held his breath to lighten all his weight,—
And lightly carried him the courtyard's length
To his own door; then, like a frightened hare,   80
Fled back in her own tracks unto her bower,
To pant awhile, and rest that all was safe.

But Charlemaign the king, who had risen by night
To look upon memorials, or at ease
To read and sign an ordinance of the realm,—   85
The Fanolehen, or Cunigosteura
For tithing corn, so to confirm the same
And stamp it with the pommel of his sword,—
Hearing their voices in the court below,
Looked from his window, and beheld the pair.   90

Angry, the king; yet laughing half to view
The strangeness and vagary of the feat;
Laughing indeed! with twenty minds to call
From his inner bed-chamber the Forty forth,
Who watched all night beside their monarch's bed,   95
With naked swords and torches in their hands,
And test this lover's-knot with steel and fire;
But with a thought, "To-morrow yet will serve
To greet these mummers," softly the window closed,
And so went back to his corn-tax again.   100

But, with the morn, the king a meeting called
Of all his lords, courtiers and kindred too,
And squire and dame,—in the great Audience Hall
Gathered; where sat the king, with the high crown
Upon his brow; beneath a drapery   105
That fell around him like a cataract!
With flecks of colour crossed and cancellate;

And over this, like trees about a stream,
Rich carven-work, heavy with wreath and rose,
Palm and palmirah, fruit and frondage, hung.   110

And more the high Hall held of rare and strange;
For on the king's right hand Leœna bowed
In cloudlike marble, and beside her crouched
The tongueless lioness; on the other side,
And poising this, the second Sappho stood,—   115
Young Erexcéa, with her head discrowned,
The anadema on the horn of her lyre;
And by the walls there hung in sequence long
Merlin himself, and Uterpendragon,
With all their mighty deeds; down to the day   120
When all the world seemed lost in wreck and rout,
A wrath of crashing steeds and men; and, in
The broken battle fighting hopelessly,
King Arthur, with the ten wounds on his head!

But not to gaze on these, appeared the peers.   125
Stern looked the king, and, when the court was met,—
The lady and her lover in the midst,—
Spoke to his lords, demanding them of this:
What merits he, the servant of the king,
Forgetful of his place, his trust, his oath,   130
Who, for his own bad end, to hide his fault,
Makes use of her, a Princess of the realm,
As of a mule;—a beast of burden!—borne
Upon her shoulders through the winter's night,
And wind and snow? "Death!" said the angry lords;   135
And knight and squire and minion murmured, "Death!"
Not one discordant voice. But Charlemaign—
Though to his foes a circulating sword,
Yet, as a king, mild, gracious, exorable,

Blest in his children too, with but one born   140
To vex his flesh like an ingrowing nail—
Looked kindly on the trembling pair, and said:
"Yes, Eginardus, well hast thou deserved
Death for this thing; for, hadst thou loved her so,
Thou shouldst have sought her Father's will in this,—   145
Protector and disposer of his child,—
And asked her hand of him, her lord and thine.
Thy life is forfeit here; but take it, thou!—
Take even two lives for this forfeit one;
And thy fair portress—wed her; honour God,   150
Love one another, and obey the king."

Thus far the legend; but of Rhotrude's smile,
Or of the lords' applause, as truly they
Would have applauded their first judgment too,
We nothing learn: yet still the story lives;   155
Shines like a light across those dark old days,
Wonderful glimpse of woman's wit and love;
And worthy to be chronicled with hers
Who to her lover dear threw down her hair,
When all the garden glanced with angry blades!   160
Or like a picture framed in battle-pikes
And bristling swords, it hangs before our view;—
The palace-court white with the fallen snow,
The good king leaning out into the night,
And Rhotrude bearing Eginard on her back.   165

Coralie.

PALE water-flowers!
That quiver in the quick turn of the brook;
    And thou, dim nook,—
Dimmer in twilight,—call again to me
Visions of life and glory that were ours   5
When first she led me here, young Coralie!

    No longer blest,
Yet standing here in silence, may not we
    Fancy or feign
That little flowers do fall about thy rest,   10
In silver mist and tender-dropping rain,
And that thy world is peace, loved Coralie?

    Our friendships flee;
And, darkening all things with her mighty shade,
    Comes Misery.   15

No longer look the faces that we see,
With the old eyes; and Woe itself shall fade,
Nor even this be left us, Coralie!

    Feelings and fears,
That once were ours, have perished in the mould,   20
    And grief is cold:
Hearts may be dead to grief; and if our tears
Are failing or forgetful, there will be
Mourners about thy bed, lost Coralie!

    The brook-flowers shine,   25
And a faint song the falling water has,
    But not for thee;
The dull night weepeth, and the sorrowing pine
Drops his dead hair upon thy young grave-grass,
    My Coralie! my Coralie!

———

I TOOK from its glass a flower,
To lay on her grave with dull accusing tears;
But the heart of the flower fell out as I handled the rose,
And my heart is shattered, and soon will wither away.

    I watch the changing shadows,   5
And the patch of windy sunshine upon the hill,
And the long blue woods; and a grief no tongue can tell,
Breaks at my eyes in drops of bitter rain.

    I hear her baby-wagon,
And the little wheels go over my heart: 10
Oh! when will the light of the darkened house return?
Oh! when will she come who made the hills so fair?

    I sit by the parlour-window
When twilight deepens, and winds get cold without;
But the blessed feet no more come up the walk,   15
And my little girl and I cry softly together.

As sometimes in a Grove.

AS sometimes in a grove at morning-chime,
        To hit his humour,
The poet lies alone, and trifles time,—
        A slow consumer;
While terebinthine tears the dark trees shed,   5
        Balsamic, grument;
And pine-straws fall into his breast, or spread
        A sere red strewment;

As come dark motions of the memory,
        Which no denial   10
Can wholly chase away; nor may we see,
        In faint espial,
The features of that doubt we brood upon
        With dull persistence,
As in broad noon our recollections run   15
        To pre-existence;

As when a man, lost on a prairie-plain
    When day is fleeting,
Looks on the glory, and then turns again,
    His steps repeating,   20
And knows not if he draws his comrades nigher,
    Nor where their camp is,
Yet turns once more to view those walls of fire
    And chrysolampis:

So idleness, and phantasy, and fear,   25
    As with dim grandeur
The night comes crowned, seem his who wanders here
    In rhyme a ranger;
Seem his, who once has seen his morning go,
    Nor dreamed it mattered;   30
Mysterious Noon; and, when the night comes, lo!
    A life well-scattered—

Is all behind; and howling wastes before:
    Oh that some warmer
Imagination might those deeps explore,   35
    And turn informer!
In the old track we paddle on, and way,
    Nor can forego it;
Or up behind that horseman of the day,
    A modern poet,   40

We mount; uncertain where we may arrive,
    Or what we trust to;
Unknowing where, indeed, our friend may drive
    His Pegasus to:
Now reining daintily by stream and sward   45
    In managed canter;

Now plunging on, thro' brick and beam and board,
    Like a Levanter!

Yet ever running on the earth his course,
    And sometimes into;   50
Chasing false fire, we fare from bad to worse;
    With such a din too—
As this that now awakes your grief and ire,
    Reader or rider—
Of halting verse; till in the Muse's mire   55
    We sink beside her.

Oh! in this day of light, must he, then, lie
    In darkness Stygian,
Who for his friend may choose Philosophy,
    Reason, Religion,   60
And find, tho' late, that creeds of good men prove
    No form or fable;
But stand on God's broad justice, and his love
    Unalterable?

Must he then, fail, because his youth went wide?   65
    Oh! hard endeavour
To gather grain from the marred mountain-side;
    Or to dissever
The lip from its old draught: we tilt the cup,
    And drug reflection;   70
Or juggle with the soul, and so patch up
    A peace or paction;

Would carry heaven with half our sins on board:
    Or, blending thickly
Earth's grosser sweet with that, to our reward   75
    Would mount up quickly;

Ready to find, when this had dimmed and shrunk,
    A more divine land,
And lightly, as a sailor climbs a trunk
    In some dark pine-land.   80

Truly a treasure in a hollow tree
    Is golden honey,
Breathing of mountain-dew, clean fragrancy,
    And uplands sunny;
But who, amid a thousand men or youth,   85
    Landward or seabred,
Would choose his honey bitter in the mouth
    With bark and bee-bread?

No! though the wish to join that harping choir
    May oft assail us,   90
We scarce shall find vague doubt, or half-desire
    Will aught avail us;
Nor fullest trust that firmest faith can get,
    Cold fear supplanting;
There may be blue and better blue, and yet   95
    Our part be wanting.

Alas! the bosom-sin, that haunts the breast,
    We pet and pension;
Or let the foolish deed still co-exist
    With fair intention.   100
From some temptation, where we did not dare,
    We turn regretful;
Yet think "the Devil finds his empty snare,"
    Not by a netful!

O conscience, coward conscience! teasing so   105
    Priest, lawyer, statist,
Thou art a cheat, and may be likened to

Least things or greatest;
A rocking-stone poised on a lonely tower
    In pastures hilly;   110
Or like an anther of that garden-flower,
    The tiger-lily;

Stirred at a breath: or stern to break and check
    All winds of heaven;
While toward some devil's-dance we crane the neck,   115
    And sigh unshriven;
Or lightly follow where our leaders go
    With pipe and tambour,
Chafing our follies till they fragrant grow,
    And like rubbed amber.   120

Yet, for these things, not godlike seems the creed
    To crush the creature,
Nor Christly sure; but shows it like indeed
    A pulpit preacher—
To fling a pebble in a pond, and roar   125
    "There! sink or swim, stone;
Get safe to land with all your ballast, or
    Black fire and brimstone!"

Ah! in a world with joy and sorrow torn,
    No life is sweeter   130
Than his, just starting in his journey's morn;
    And seems it bitter
To give up all things for the pilgrim's staff,
    And garment scanty;
The moonlight-walk, the dream, the dance, the laugh,   135
    And fair Rhodanthe!

And must it be, when but to him, in truth,
    Whom it concerneth,

The spirit speaks? Yet to the tender tooth
    The tongue still turneth.   140
And he, who proudly walks through life, and hears
    Pæan and plaudit,
Looks ever to the end with doubts and fears,
    And that last audit.

But, as we sometimes see before the dawn,   145
    With motion gentle,
Across the lifeless landscape softly drawn
    A misty mantle;
Up from the river to the bluffs away,
    The low land blurring,   150
All dim and still, and in the broken gray
    Some faint stars stirring:

So, when the shadow falls across our eyes,
    And interveneth
A veil 'twixt us and all we know and prize;   155
    Then, in the zenith,
May heaven's lone lights not pass in wreaths obscure,
    But, still sojourning
Amid the cloud, appoint us to the pure
    And perfect morning!   160

And even here,—when stretching wide our hands,
    Longing and leaning,
To find, 'mid jarring aims and fierce demands,
    Our strength and meaning;
Though troubled to its depths the spirit heaves,   165
    Though dim despairing,—
Shall we not find Life's mesh of wreck and leaves
    Pale pearls insnaring?

Yes:—as the waters cast upon the land
    Loose dulse and laver,   170

And where the sea beats in, befringe the sand
    With wild sea-slaver;—
For currents lift the laden and the light,
    Ground-swell and breaker;
Not weedy trash alone, but corallite,   175
    Jasper, and nacre.

And though at times the tempter sacks our souls,
    And fiends usurp us,
Let us still press for right, as ocean rolls,
    Wtih power and purpose;   180
Returning still, though backward flung and foiled,
    To higher station,
So to work out, distained and sorely soiled,
    Our own salvation.

Nor following Folly's lamp, nor Learning's lore,   185
    But, humbly falling
Before our Father and our Friend, implore
    Our gift and calling.
Outside the vineyard we have wandered long
    In storm and winter: 190
Oh! guide the grasping hands, the footsteps wrong,
    And bid us enter—

Ere the day draw to dark; nor heave and prize
    With strength unable,
Nor range a world for wisdom's fruit, that lies   195
    On our own table.
So shall we find each movement an advance,
    Each hour momentous,
If but, in our own place and circumstance,
    Thou, God, content us.   200

Mark Atherton.

OF one who went to do deliberate wrong;
Not driven by want, nor hard necessity,
Nor seemingly impelled by hidden hands
As some have said; nor hounded on by hate,
Imperious anger, nor the lust of gold,   5
This story tells. Yet all of these colleagued
To drive him at the last; who in young life,
Ere the bone hardens, or the blood grows cold,
When youth is prompt to change, even momently,
With every whiff of wind, or word of chance,—   10
Through heat and cold, for many a month and day
Went calmly to his purpose with still feet;
No break-neck speed, but fearfully, and as one
Who holds his horse together down a hill.

Bethiah, or, as those who loved her loved   15
To call her, Bertha, for her beauty's sake,—

Bethiah Westbrooke was a forest-flower,
That trembled forth on the waste woods and swamps
Of wild New England, in the wild dark days
Of witchcraft, and of Indian wiles and war.   20
Yet something after this; for oft at night,
When Westbrooke's cottage was a beacon-star
To many a beating heart, and suitors came
From far with gifts and game, then the old man,
Who felt the fire, and had a gust to talk,   25
Would tell of Philip's war and Sassacus;
And how De Rouville crossed the crusted snow
Towards doomed Deerfield in the winter's morn,—
With a quick rush and halt alternately,
As 'twere the empty rushing of the wind,   30
So to delude the outposts; how by night,
About the lonely blockhouse and the mount,
The scouting Indian hovered like a wolf,
Seeking a crevice to thrust in the fire;
Till the dumb creatures of the barn and field   35
Would give swift notice of the stealing foe;
Cows, horses, snuffed the war-paint; and, in the house,
How the dog whimpered with erected hair,
And, like the wind in a window, wawled the cat.
Of these, and personal scapes, would Westbrooke speak   40
As of the past: "For now," he said, "the tribes,
Shot, scalped, and scattered, flee on every side;
Their bark-boats staved and sunk, their lodges burned,
And plantings, and even the lands that grew them, seized,
They scarce can draw to head. The Indian war   45
Was ended; save that, perhaps, in the long nights,
From some lone farm outlying, a fire might rise,
Set on by the wild savage with a shriek!
For squads were here and there; and still 'twas said,
That in the North some stragglers held together;   50

But mainly broken now; nor seemed it best
To mull and grind them into very dust."

And then the old man, turning, as he talked,
Towards his daughter, bitterly would speak
Of that most hateful sin of treachery;   55
False friendliness, and that domestic treason,
Wherein the red man, trustless, merciless,
Is better than the white; then, pausing long,
Would gaze upon Bethiah where she sat,
Till the girl winced, and on her forehead stood   60
The impatient colour; and Mark, Mark Atherton,
Into his dark avoiding eye would seem
To call a clear look, till the old man's fell.
Not lovers these, though long-accounted friends;
And, though the voice went that they two would wed,   65
Not lovers sure: yet the youth had her ear
And ready laughter; for he well could speak
Smooth words, but with an edge of meaning in them,
Like a sharp acid sheathed in milk or oil.
Others, too, held aloof; but yet the maid   70
Heard not, or, hearing, heard with a half-heart;
For still another stood between the two,—
Companion of the twilights and the dawns
Of parted days; one who had loved her then
With true-intending love,—his hope, his star,   75
And almost mistress! And so the maiden looked
On this and this, with a divided eye.

Into the forest rode Mark Atherton.
Leaving the settlement at the river-side,
By felling and burnt-over land he passed, and plunged   80
Thro' towering fern and thickset, till he reached
The open pines; and onward still he rode;
Climbing the slippery slope, and clattering down

The stony hollow. From his horse's hoof
The shy frog flew; and, like a streak of light,   85
The squirrel darted up the mossy bole,
Where, glancing upward, downward, and across,
Hammered and hung the crested popinjay.

So sharply on he rode; now brooding on
His purpose, which was in truth to win the maid,   90
Wrong her rich love, and sell her to the chiefs
That lurked with their red warriors in the shade;
Now on her beauty with a grain of ruth,
Their long-time friendship, and that marriage-vow
Which his heart hated: for he thought of one,   95
Once the heart's idol of his boyish dream,
That hardly heaven seemed fitted to enshrine;
Now pent within a house just bigger than
A martin-box, that seemed, and scarce as clean,—
The fair slight girl that was,—"And see her now!   100
A dozen children at her gown-tail pull,
As so a slut as ere went down-at-heel!"

So, hardening his heart, he drew his rein
Against the bank, and sought the water-side;
Parting the laurel to behold thy face,   105
New England's Stream, cold River of the Pines!
There lay and listened till the twilight fell;
When, weary of the flutter of the leaf,
The dipping of the ripple on the rock,
And plaintive calling of the phœbe-bird,   110
He chanted, half-in-fear, half mockingly:—

    "The river-sides are high, are high, the night is dark!
    And fair white hands are drawing at our bark:
    To-night, to-night, the winds obey our call,
    And the still, dark river sucks like a waterfall,   115

As downstream in the dug-out on we fare;
For the minister's daughter, and deacon's wife are there.
        Paddle away!

On either bank, as softly, softly down she plies,
Remember, remember, that many a landing lies: 120
Then fear not the Friend, with whom we have our part;
Nor shame to own the love that hideth in the heart;
Nor grudge our chiefest chamber to afford,
When the house is his from sill to saddle-board;
        Paddle away!"   125

        And with the cadence came
The quick replying plunge of a broad blade;
And, hideous in his paint and peag, with face
Inflexible of mournful gravity,
An Indian chieftain, leaping from his boat,   130
Stood, like the fiend evoked. But Atherton,
Whose cheek had whitened like the winter-leaf
That flickers all day in the whistling beech,
Held down his head as for a moment, so
Recovering his face; then steadfastly   135
Exchanged due greeting with the forest-king,
And passed they into parley by the stream.

Red light had parted from the westward verge,
And night lay black, ere back again and fast
The horseman fled, a shadow through the shade.   140
And now indeed, as if in very truth,
The river-demons gathered on his track;
For, ever as he rode, a woman's shriek
Seemed to pursue him through the sounding pines!
And where he looked, there, was a woman's face,   145
With the frothed lip, and nostril edged with blood,

Relentlessly appealing, as it seemed.
And, ever as he rode, a ceaseless sound
Went ringing at his ear like jingling gold;
And, like the innumerable chink and chime   150
Of the night-crickets hidden in the grass,
Not to be lost or left; he gnashed his teeth:
But even there the forest fell away,
And on, by burned and blackened stumps and shells,
That mimicked all things horrible and vague,   155
In the dim glimmer insecure, he sped,
And gained the pickets of the palisade.

Another night, and later in the year,
A youth and maid, in the first edge of dark,
Stood by the haunted stream, or wandered on;   160
Insensibly approaching in their talk
A bushy point that jutted from the wood;—
Alley and ambuscade of black pitch-pine.
Various their look: he, lowering in his mood,
Baffled and broken where his heart was high,   165
Strode sullenly; she, sad, but resolute,
And pale with her determination; yet
As one who strives to soothe a cureless harm,
Spoke tenderly, as to an angry friend;
Remembering old affection ere he go.   170
"Partings must be," she said; "but is not this
A sorrowful leavetaking to our love,—
To all our friendliness an ill farewell?"
A moment more, and while the words were warm,
Torn from her feet, arms bound, and gagged with grass,   175
They trailed her through the thickets of the wood.
And all alone stood Atherton,—with him
The sachem of the riverside and stream;—

Receiving now, what he had had in part,
All the bad wage of his iniquity.   180
Then, as if all things now were at an end,
Released from gift of faith, and entergage,
They parted silent: one took up the trail,
The other slowly to the village passed,
And raised the alarm, and blew the gathering-horn,   185
And headed the wild search.
                       With trampling feet
He led them to the River, where, he said,
They dragged her through the stream, and up the bank,
He following on into its very flow;
But his foot slipping in the anchor-ice,   190
With wetted gun, and bruised among the stones,
He saw her, for whose life he risked his own,
Snatched from his sight: but darker now the night,
They far before, the trail unsure by day,
What more could be, but gather arms and men,   195
And scout abroad, and watch, till morning light?

And Westbrooke, the old man without a child,
Now raging, now in blank and mute despair,
Ran forth, or stood in helplessness of grief:
Not now as when he marched with Mosely's men   200
Against the savage seated in his strength!
When, like a sword of fire, with twenty more,
He fell upon their necks, and drove them in;
Or under Winslow, in that desperate day,
When, beaten off by the red foe intrenched,   205
Through battle-smoke he found himself alone
O'er breastwork and abbatis charging back.
Gone was his strength; and, as the days went by,
Gone seemed his heart. He sought his bed, and there
Seeing but one face, as the days went by,   210

Lay motionless, and like a drowning man,
Who, lying at the bottom of a brook,
Stares at the sun; till, small and smaller grown,
It flickers like a lamp, and then,—goes out;
So shrank his hope, so dropped into the dark.   215

And days went by, and still no tidings were.
The smouldered war broke up in fresher flame,
Killing all hope; the rangers, ranging back
Through all the Massachusetts, west and north,
Had swept the woods to farthest Canada,   220
And many prisoners ransomed or retook:
But she, the glory of his life, was gone.
And yet, one winter morning, ere the sun
Had crossed the river on his westward march,
Sudden as was the stroke, the mercy came;   225
And Westbrooke held the daughter of his heart;
Wilted and wan, yet still the Forest-Flower!
Brought by the party of a friendly tribe,
Who took her from the chiefs, sick unto death;
And nursed her long, and tenderly led her home,   230
Nor claimed reward.
                      And sudden vengeance broke
On him, the traitor; but not by those he had wronged:
Fled on the instant to the cedar-swamps,
His Indian allies seized and bound him there;
And after battle, chafing for their slain,   235
There, in the darkness of the cedar-swamp,
They slowly burned his flesh, and charred his bones.

So, in the old days, God was over all!
Vengeance was full, and wrong returned to right;
Mercy replied to Love; the lost was found;   240
And treachery answered so with treachery.

Sidney.

HAVE you forgotten that still afternoon,
How fair the fields were, and the brooks how full?
The hills how happy in their hanging green?
The fields were green; and here, in spots and holes
Where the rich rain had settled, greener green.   5
We sat beside a window to the south,
Talking of nothing, or in silence sat,
Till, weary of the summer-darkened room,
I in an impulse spoke, you smiled; and so
In this consent we wandered forth together   10
Across the fields to entertain the time.

Shall I retrace those steps until we reach
Again the crossing River? Yes; for so
Again I seem to tread those paths with you:
Here are the garden-beds, the shrubbery,   15

And moody murmur of the poising bee;
And here the hedge that to the River runs.
Beside me still you mov'd thro' meadow-flowers;
Beside, yet unapproached; cold as a star
On the morning's purple brink; and seemingly 20
Unconscious of the world beneath your feet.
Yet as I plucked up handfuls from the grass,
With here and there a flower, telling their names
And talking ignorant words of why they were,
You paused to gather berries from the hedge; 25
And I despaired to reach you with my words,
Believed you cold, nor wished to find myself
Calling your face back, and as in a dream
Lingering about the places where you were;
And would not if I might, or so it seemed, 30
Attain unto the property of your love:
Knowing full well that I must soon awake,
Gaze blankly round, and, with a bottomless sigh,
Relapse into my life;—the life I knew
Before I saw your fair hair softly put 35
From off your temples, and the parted mouth,—
More beautiful indeed, than any flower,
Half-open, and expectant of the rain.
O youth and loveliness! are ye less dear
Placed at impracticable height, or where 40
Not wholly clear, but touched with shades and spots
Of coldness and caprice? or do such make
The bright more bright, as sometimes we may see
In the old pictures? Is the knight's brow held
Not noble for its scar? or she less fair, 45
The lady with the lozenge on her lip?
So may your very failings grace you more;
And I, most foolish in my wisdom, find

The grapes alone are sour we cannot gain.
But, Sidney, look! the River runs below,—   50
Dark-channelled Deerfield, here beneath our feet,
Unfordable,—a natural bar and stay.
Yet, ere you turn, let us look off together,
As travellers from a hill; not separate yet,
But being to be divided, let us look   55
Upon the mountains and the summer sky;
The meadow with the herd in its green heart;
The ripple, and the rye-grass on the bank,
As what we ne'er may so behold again.
And, do me right in this, the eye, that saw   60
These accidents and adjuncts, could not fail
To mark you, loveliest of the place and time;
A separate beauty, which was yet akin
To all soft graces of the earth and sky,
While wanting naught that human warmth could give.   65
So, lady, take the bitter from my words:
Let us go onward now; and should you prize
In any way the homage of a heart
Most desolate of love, that finds in all
Still the salt taste of tears, receive it here,   70
With aught that I can give, or you retain.
Let me, though turning backward with dim eyes,
Recover from the past one golden look,
Remembering this valley of the stream;
And the sweet presence that gave light on all,   75
And my injustice, and indeed your scorn,
Refusing me the half-stripped clover-stalk
Your fingers picked to pieces as we walked.
Yet, ere we part, take from my lips this wish,—
Not from my lips alone, from my heart's midst,—   80
That your young life may be undimmed with storms,

Nor the wind beat, nor wild rain lash it out,
But over change and sorrow rise and ride!
Leading o'er all a tranquil, lenient light;
And, when your evening comes, around that beam   85
No tragic twilight brood, but late and long
Your crystal beauty linger like a star,—
Like a pure poignant star in the fleecy pink.

But give your poet now one perfect flower:
For here we reach again the garden's bound,—   90
Sweet as yourself, and of one lustre too;
Yet not the red dark bud Damascus yields,
Nor York-and-Lancaster, nor white, nor yellow,
But a rose-coloured rose.

Refrigerium.

LET them lie,—their day is over;
  Only night and stillness be:
Let the slow rain come, and bring
  Brake and star-grass, speedwell, harebell,
All the fulness of the spring;   5
  What reck I of friend and lover?
Foe by foe laid lovingly?

What are mounds of green earth, either?
  What, to me, unfriendly bones
Death hath pacified and won   10
  To a reconcilèd patience,
Though their very graves have run
  In the blending earth together,
And the spider links the stones?

To the hills I wander, crying,— 15
   Where we stood in days of old,
Stood and saw the sunset die;
   Watched through tears the passing purple,—
"O my darling! misery
   Has been mine; but thou wert lying 20
In a slumber sweet and cold."

Sonnets. PART I.

I.

SOMETIMES, when winding slow by brook and bower,
Beating the idle grass,—of what avail,
I ask, are these dim fancies, cares, and fears?
What though from every bank I drew a flower,—
Bloodroot, king-orchis, or the pearlwort pale,—   5
And set it in my verse with thoughtful tears?
What would it count, though I should sing my death,
And muse and mourn with as poetic breath
As, in damp garden walks, the autumn gale
Sighs o'er the fallen floriage? What avail   10
Is the swan's voice, if all the hearers fail?
Or his great flight, that no eye gathereth,
In the blending blue? And yet, depending so,
God were not God, whom knowledge cannot know.

II.

WHEREFORE, with this belief, held like a blade,—
Gathering my strength and purpose, fair and slow,
I wait; resolved to carry it to the heart
Of that dark doubt in one collected blow;
And stand at guard with spirit undismayed, 5
Nor fear the Opposer's anger, arms, or art;
When, from a hiding near, behold him start
With a fresh weapon of my weakness made;
And goad me with myself, and urge the attack,
While I strike short, and still give back and back 10
While the foe rages. Then from that disgrace
He points to where they sit that have won the race,
Laurel by laurel wreathing, face o'er face,
And leaves me lower still; for, ranked in place,

III.

AND borne with theirs, my proudest thoughts do seem
Bald at the best, and dim; a barren gleam
Among the immortal stars, and faint and brief
As north-light flitting in the dreary north.
"What have thy dreams,—a vague, prospective worth? 5
An import imminent? or dost thou deem
Thy life so fair, that thou wouldst set it forth
Before the day? or art thou wise in grief,
Has fruitful Sorrow swept thee with her wing?"
To-day I heard a sweet voice carolling 10
In the wood-land paths, with laugh and careless cry,
Leading her happy mates. Apart I stept;
And, while the laugh and song went lightly by,
In the wild bushes I sat down and wept.

IV.

NOR looks that backward life so bare to me,
My later youth, and ways I've wandered through;
But touched with innocent grace,—the early bee
On the maple log, the white-heaped cherry-tree
That hummed all day in the sun, the April blue!   5
Yet hardly now one ray the Forward hath
To show where sorrow rests, and rest begins;
Although I check my feet, nor walk to wrath
Through days of crime, and grosser shadowings
Of evil done in the dark; but fearfully,   10
Mid unfulfilled yet unrelinquished sins
That hedge me in, and press about my path,
Like purple-poison flowers of stramony,
With their dull opiate-breath, and dragon-wings.

V.

AND so the day drops by; the horizon draws
The fading sun, and we stand struck in grief;
Failing to find our haven of relief,—
Wide of the way, nor sure to turn or pause;
And weep to view how fast the splendour wanes,   5
And scarcely heed, that yet some share remains
Of the red after-light, some time to mark,
Some space between the sundown and the dark.
But not for him those golden calms succeed,
Who, while the day is high, and glory reigns,   10
Sees it go by,—as the dim Pampas plain,
Hoary with salt, and gray with bitter weed,
Sees the vault blacken, feels the dark wind strain,
Hears the dry thunder roll, and knows no rain.

VI.

NOT sometimes, but, to him that heeds the whole,
And in the Ample reads his personal page,
Labouring to reconcile, content, assuage,
The vexed conditions of his heritage,
For ever waits an angel at the goal;   5
and ills seem but as food for spirits sage,
And grief becomes a dim apparelage,
The weed and wearing of the sacred soul.
Might I but count, but here, one watchlight spark!
But vain, oh vain! this turning for the light,—   10
Vain as a groping hand to rend the dark.
I call, entangled in the night,—a night
Of wind and voices! but the gusty roll
Is vague, nor comes there cheer of pilotage.

VII.

DANK fens of cedar; hemlock-branches gray
With tress and trail of mosses wringing-wet;
Beds of the black pitch-pine in dead leaves set
Whose wasted red has wasted to white away;
Remnants of rain, and droppings of decay,—   5
Why hold ye so my heart, nor dimly let
Through your deep leaves the light of yesterday,
The faded glimmer of a sunshine set?
Is it that in your blindness, shut from strife,
The bread of tears becomes the bread of life?   10
Far from the roar of day, beneath your boughs
Fresh griefs beat tranquilly, and loves and vows
Grow green in your gray shadows, dearer far
Even than all lovely lights, and roses, are?

VIII.

AS when, down some broad River dropping, we,
Day after day, behold the assuming shores
Sink and grow dim, as the great Water-course
Pushes his banks apart and seeks the sea;
Benches of pines, high shelf and balcony,   5
To flats of willow and low sycamores
Subsiding, till, where'er the wave we see,
Himself is his horizon utterly:
So fades the portion of our early world.
Still on the ambit hangs the purple air;   10
Yet, while we lean to read the secret there,
The stream that by green shore-sides plashed and purled
Expands; the mountains melt to vapors rare,
And life alone circles out flat and bare.

IX.

YET wear we on; the deep light disallowed
That lit our youth,—in years no longer young,
We wander silently, and brood among
Dead graves, and tease the sun-break and the cloud
For import. Were it not better yet to fly,   5
To follow those who go before the throng,
Reasoning from stone to star, and easily
Exampling this existence? or shall I—
Who yield slow reverence where I cannot see,
And gather gleams, where'er by chance or choice   10
My footsteps draw,—though brokenly dispensed,—
Come into light at last? or suddenly,
Struck to the knees like Saul, one arm against
The overbearing brightness, hear—a Voice?

X.

AN upper chamber in a darkened house,
Where, ere his footsteps reached ripe manhood's brink,
Terror and anguish were his cup to drink,—
I cannot rid the thought, nor hold it close;
But dimly dream upon that man alone;—   5
Now though the autumn clouds most softly pass;
The cricket chides beneath the doorstep stone,
And greener than the season grows the grass.
Nor can I drop my lids, nor shade my brows,
But there he stands beside the lifted sash;   10
And, with a swooning of the heart, I think
Where the black shingles slope to meet the boughs,
And—shattered on the roof like smallest snows—
The tiny petals of the mountain-ash.

XI.

WHAT profits it to me, though here allowed
Life, sunlight, leisure, if they fail to urge
Me to due motion, or myself to merge
With the onward stream, too humble, or too proud?
That find myself not with the popular surge   5
Washed off and on, or up to higher reefs
Flung with the foremost, when the rolling crowd
Hoists like a wave, nor strong to speak aloud;
But standing here, gazing on my own griefs,
Strange household woe, and wounds that bleed and smart; 10
With still lips, and an outcry in the heart!—
Or now, from day to day, I coldly creep
By summer farms and fields, by stream and steep,
Dull, and like one exhausted with deep sleep.

XII.

TALL, stately plants, with spikes and forks of gold,
Crowd every slope: my heart repeats its cry,—
A cry for strength, for strength and victory;
The will to strive, the courage overbold
That would have moved me once to turn indeed,   5
And level with the dust each lordly weed.
But now I weep upon my wayside walks,
And sigh for those fair days, when glorying
I stood a boy amid the mullein-stalks,
And dreamed myself like him the Lion-King;   10
There, where his shield shed arrows, and the clank
Clashed on his helm of battle-axe and brand,
He pushed the battle backward, rank on rank,
Fallen in the sword-swing of his stormy hand.

XIII.

AS one who walks and weeps by alien brine,
And hears the heavy land-wash break, so I,
Apart from friends, remote in misery,
But brood on pain, and find in heaven no sign:
The lights are strange, and bitter voices by.   5
So the doomed sailor, left alone to die,
Looks sadly seaward at the day's decline,
And hears his parting comrades' jeers and scoffs;
Or sees, through mists that hinder and deform,
The dewy stars of home,—sees Regulus shine   10
With a hot flicker through the murky damp,
And setting Sirius twitch and twinge like a lamp
Slung to the mast-head, in a night of storm,
Of lonely vessel labouring in the troughs.

XIV.

NOT proud of station, nor in worldly pelf
Immoderately rich, nor rudely gay;
Gentle he was, and generous in a way,
And with a wise direction ruled himself.
Large Nature spread his table every day;   5
And so he lived,—to all the blasts that woo,
Responsible, as yon long locust spray
That waves and washes in the windy blue.
Nor wanted he a power to reach and reap
From hardest things a consequence and use;   10
And yet this friend of mine, in one small hour
Fell from himself, and was content to weep
For eyes love-dark, red lips, and cheeks in hues
Not red, but rose-dim, like the jacinth-flower!

XV.

AND she, her beauty never made her cold,—
Young-Oread-like, beside the green hill-crest,
And blissfully obeying Love's behest,
She turned to him as to a god of old!
Her smitten soul with its full strength and spring   5
Retaliating his love: unto that breast,
Ere scarce the arms dared open to infold,
She gave herself as but a little thing!
And now,—to impulse cold, to passion dead,—
With the wild grief of unperfected years,   10
He kissed her hands, her mouth, her hair, her head;
Gathered her close and closer, to drink up
The odour of her beauty; then in tears,
As for a world, gave from his lips the cup!

XVI.

YET Nature, where the thunder leaves its trace
On the high hemlock pine, or sandstone bank,
Hating all shock of hue, or contrast rank,
With some consenting colour heals the place,
Or o'er it draws her mosses green and dank.   5
So gentle Time will bring with tender craft
Another day, and other greens ingraft
On the dead soil, so fire-burned now, and blank.
What we have had, we hold; and cannot sink
Remembrance: patience cometh from above.   10
And now he breathes apart, to daily drink
In tears the bitter ashes of his love,
Yet precious-rich, and a diviner draught
Than Agria or Artemisia drank!

XVII.

ALL men,—the Preacher saith,—whate'er or whence
Their increase, walking thro' this world has been;
Both those that gather out, or after-glean,
Or hold in simple fee of harvests dense;
Or but perhaps a flowerless barren green,   5
Barren with spots of sorrel, knot-grass, spurge:—
See to one end their differing paths converge,
And all must render answer, here or hence.
"Lo! Death is at the doors," he crieth, "with blows!"
But what to him, unto whose feverish sense   10
The stars tick audibly, and the wind's low surge
In the pine, attended, tolls, and throngs, and grows
On the dread ear,—a thunder too profound
For bearing,—a Niagara of sound!

XVIII.

PERCHANCE his own small field some charge demands,—
So full the eternal Choral sobs and swells;
But clear away the weeds, although there lurk
Within the weeds a few dim asphodels,
Flowers of a former day, how fair! how fair!   5
And yet behold them not, but to the work,
Before the short light darken, set thy hands!
Nor over the surface dip with easy share,
But beam-deep, plough and plunge your parallels,
Breaking in clod and flower! that so may spring   10
From the deep grain a goodlier growth and kind;
Unstirred of heats that blast, of frosts that bind,
Nor swept aside, ere the seed catch, by wing
Of casual shower, nor any chance of wind.

XIX.

YET vain, perhaps, the fruits our care applaud:
If the Fore-fate decree the harvest fat,
Why should we mind this thing, or matter that,
To sift the seed, and blow the chaff abroad?
But doubt not so the Giver to defraud,   5
Who will accuse thy labour: spend, nor slack
Of thy best strength and sweetness too, till God,
With a full hand and flowing, pay thee back.
Behold! on rolling zone and zodiac
The spray and scatter of his bounty flung!   10
And what canst thou, to whom no hands belong
To hasten by one hour the morning's birth?
Or stay one planet at his circle hung,
In the great flight of stars across the earth?

XX.

STILL craves the spirit: never Nature solves
That yearning which with her first breath began;
And, in its blinder instinct, still devolves
On god or pagod, Manada or man,
Or, lower yet, brute-service, apes and wolves!   5
By Borneo's surf, the bare Barbarian
Still to the sands beneath him bows to pray:
Give Greek his god, the Bheel his devil-sway;
And what remains to me, who count no odds
Between such Lord and him I saw to-day,—   10
The farmer mounted on his market-load,
Bundles of wool, and locks of upland hay;
The son of toil, that his own works bestrode,
And him, Ophion, earliest of the gods?

XXI.

O FATHER, God! to whom, in happier days,
My father bade me cry when troubles fall,
Again I come before thy tribunal,
Too faint for prayer, and all too blind for praise;
Yet owning never, through life's dim career,   5
The eye that would not see, and reckless ear;
Against my head no more thy tempests call!—
Refreshing that wild sorrow of the heart,
And those fierce tears: another morning raise
Upon this vision, now so dimmed and swoln: 10
Guide me, as once, unto thy feet to flee;
Claiming no price of labour, place, or part;
And only seek, before thy footstool fall'n,
Tears in mine eyes, to lift these hands of me!

XXII.

THE morning comes; not slow, with reddening gold,
But wildly driven, with windy shower, and sway
As though the wind would blow the dark away!
Voices of wail, of misery multifold,
Wake with the light, and its harsh glare obey;   5
And yet I walk betimes this day of spring,
Still my own private portion reckoning,
Not to compute, though every tear be told.
Oh, might I on the gale my sorrow fling!
But sweep, sweep on, wild blast! who bids thee stay?   10
Across the stormy headlands shriek and sing;
And, earlier than the daytime, bring the day
To pouring eyes, half-quenched with watery sight,
And breaking hearts that hate the morning light!

XXIII.

SHALL I not see her? Yes: for one has seen
Her in her beauty, since we called her dead,—
One like herself, a fair young mother, led
By her own lot to feel compassion keen;
And unto her last night my Anna came,   5
And sat within her arms, and spoke her name,
"While the old smile," she said, "like starlight gleamed:
And like herself in fair young bloom," she said,
"Only the white more white, the red more red;
And fainter than the mist her pressure seemed."   10
And words there were, though vague, yet beautiful,
Which she who heard them could not tell to me;—
It is enough! my Anna did not flee
To grief or fear, nor lies in slumber dull.

XXIV.

PERHAPS a dream; yet surely truth has beamed
Oft from the gate of dreams upon the brain;
As on yon mountain, black with thunder-rain,
To-day, through cloudy clefts, the glory streamed.
Why do men doubt, and balance, and disdain,   5
Where she, the gentler spirit, seeks to skim
Light from the vague,—though thick the shadows swim;
Still counting what she may not all explain,—
Not to be lost, or lightly disesteemed,—
Though cloudy of shape it seem, and meaning dim?   10
Did Manoah's wife doubt ere she showed to him
The angel standing in the golden grain?
Had Deborah fear? or was that Vision vain
That Actia, Arlotte, and Mandané dreamed?

XXV.

BY this low fire I often sit to woo
Memory to bring the days for ever done;
And call the mountains, where our love begun,
And the dear happy woodlands dipped in dew;
And pore upon the landscape, like a book,   5
But cannot find her: or there rise to me
Gardens and groves in light and shadow outspread:
Or, on a headland far away, I see
Men marching slow in orderly review;
And bayonets flash, as, wheeling from the sun,   10
Rank after rank give fire: or, sad, I look
On miles of moonlit brine, with many a bed
Of wave-weed heaving,—there, the wet sands shine,
And just awash, the low reef lifts its line.

XXVI.

FOR Nature daily through her grand design
Breathes contradiction where she seems most clear:
For I have held of her the gift to hear;
And felt, indeed, endowed of sense divine,
When I have found, by guarded insight fine,   5
Cold April flowers in the green end of June;
And thought myself possessed of Nature's ear,
When, by the lonely mill-brook, into mine,
Seated on slab, or trunk asunder sawn,
The night-hawk blew his horn at sunny noon;   10
And in the rainy midnight I have heard
The ground-sparrow's long twitter from the pine,
And the cat-bird's silver song,—the wakeful bird
That to the lighted window sings for dawn.

XXVII.

SO, to the mind long brooding but on it—
A haunting theme for anger, joy, or tears,—
With ardent eyes, not what we think, appears,
But, hunted home, behold its opposite!
Worn Sorrow breaking in disastrous mirth,   5
And wild tears wept of laughter, like the drops
Shook by the trampling thunder to the earth;
And each seems either, or but a counterfeit
Of that it would dissemble: hopes are fears,
And love is woe. Nor here the discord stops;   10
But through all human life runs the account,—
Born into pain, and ending bitterly;
Yet sweet perchance, between-time, like a fount,
That rises salt, and freshens to the sea.

XXVIII.

NOT the round natural world, not the deep mind,
The reconcilement holds: the blue abyss
Collects it not; our arrows sink amiss;
And but in Him may we our import find.
The agony to know, the grief, the bliss   5
Of toil, is vain and vain! clots of the sod
Gathered in heat and haste, and flung behind
To blind ourselves and others,—what but this
Still grasping dust, and sowing toward the wind?
No more thy meaning seek, thine anguish plead;   10
But, leaving straining thought, and stammering word,
Across the barren azure pass to God;
Shooting the void in silence, like a bird,—
A bird that shuts his wings for better speed!

Sonnets. PART II.

I.

"THAT boy,"—the farmer said, with hazel wand
Pointing him out, half by the haycock hid,—
"Though bare sixteen, can work at what he's bid,
From sun till set,—to cradle, reap, or band."
I heard the words, but scarce could understand   5
Whether they claimed a smile, or gave me pain;
Or was it aught to me, in that green lane,
That all day yesterday, the briers amid,
He held the plough against the jarring land
Steady, or kept his place among the mowers;   10
Whilst other fingers, sweeping for the flowers,
Brought from the forest back a crimson stain?
Was it a thorn that touched the flesh? or did
The poke-berry spit purple on my hand?

II.

NOR idle all, though naught he sees in thine—
But dallying with the day to make it brief;
And thinks it braver far to tramp the leaf
With dog and gun, thro' tamerac, birch, and pine;
Or lounge the day beneath a tavern-sign: 5
Yet in *his* labour can I well discern
Great workings moving, both in his, and mine.
What though indeed a joyless verse I turn?
The flowers are fair, and give their glimmering heaps
To grace her rest. And so to-night I pass   10
To that low mound, gone over now with grass,
And find her stirless still; whilst overhead
Creation moveth, and the farm-boy sleeps
A still strong sleep, till but the east is red.

III.

YES: though the brine may from the desert deep
Run itself sweet before it finds the foam,
Oh! what for him—the deep heart once a home
For love and light—is left?—to walk and weep;
Still, with astonished sorrow, watch to keep   5
On his dead day: he weeps, and knows his doom,
Yet standeth stunned; as one who climbs a steep,
And dreaming softly of the cottage-room,
The faces round the porch, the rose in showers,—
Gains the last height between his heart and it;   10
And, from the windows where his children sleep,
Sees the red fire fork; or, later come,
Finds, where he left his home, a smouldering pit,—
Blackness and scalding stench, for love and flowers!

IV.

BUT Grief finds solace faint in others' ills,
And but in her own shadow loves to go:
For her, the mountain-side may flower or flow;
Alike to that dull eye, the wild brook fills
With mist the chasm, or feeds the fields below;   5
Alike the latter rain, with sure return,
Breaks in the barren pine, or thick distils
On the pond-lily and the green brook flags,
Or rises softly up to flood the fern.
What though the world were water-drowned? or though   10
The sun, from his high place descending slow,
Should over the autumn landscapes brood and burn,
Till all the vales were tinder, and their crags,
Apt to the touch of fire, Hephæstian hills?

V.

NO shame dissuades his thought, no scorn despoils
Of beauty, who, the daily heaven beneath,
Gathers his bread by run-sides, rocks, and groves.
He drinks from rivers of a thousand soils;
And, where broad Nature blows, he takes his breath: 5
For so his thought stands like the things he loves,
In thunderous purple like Cascadnac peak,
Or glimpses faint with grass and cinquefoils.
The friend may listen with a sneering cheek,
Concede the matter good, and wish good luck;   10
Or plainly say, "Your brain is planet-struck!"—
And drop your hoarded thought as vague and vain,
Like bypast flowers, to redden again in rain,
Flung to the offal-heap with shard and shuck!

VI.

NO! cover not the fault. The wise revere
The judgment of the simple: harshly flow
The words of counsel; but the end may show
Matter and music to the unwilling ear.
But perfect grief, like love, should cast out fear,   5
And, like an o'er-brimmed river, moaning go.
Yet shrinks it from the senseless chaff and chat
Of those who smile, and insolently bestow
Their ignorant praise; or those who stoop and peer
To pick with sharpened fingers for a flaw;   10
Nor ever touch the quick, nor rub the raw.
Better than this, were surgery rough as that,
Which, hammer and chisel in hand, at one sharp blow
Strikes out the wild tooth from a horse's jaw!

VII.

HIS heart was in his garden; but his brain
Wandered at will among the fiery stars:
Bards, heroes, prophets, Homers, Hamilcars,
With many angels, stood, his eye to gain;
The devils, too, were his familiars.   5
And yet the cunning florist held his eyes
Close to the ground,—a tulip-bulb his prize,—
And talked of tan and bone-dust, cutworms, grubs,
As though all Nature held no higher strain;
Or, if he spoke of Art, he made the theme   10
Flow through box-borders, turf, and flower-tubs;
Or, like a garden-engine's, steered the stream,—
Now spouted rainbows to the silent skies;
Now kept it flat, and raked the walks and shrubs.

VIII.

COMPANIONS were we in the grove and glen!
Through belts of summer wandered hour on hour,
Ransacking sward and swamp to deck his bower,—
River, and reservoir of mountain rain;
Nor sought for hard-named herb, or plant of power,   5
But Whippoorwill-shoe, and quaint Sidesaddle-flower.
And still he talked, asserting, thought is free;
And wisest souls by their own action shine:
"For beauty," he said, "is seen where'er we look,
Growing alike in waste and guarded ground;   10
And, like the May-flower, gathered equally
On desolate hills, where scantily the pine
Drops his dry wisps about the barren rock,
And in the angles of the fences found."

IX.

BUT unto him came swift calamity,
In the sweet spring-time, when his beds were green;
And my heart waited, trustfully serene,
For the new blossom on my household-tree.
But flowers, and gods, and quaint Philosophy,   5
Are poor, in truth, to fill the empty place;
Nor any joy, nor season's jollity,
Can aught, indeed, avail to grace our grief.
Can spring return to him a brother's face?
Or bring my darling back to me,—to me?   10
Undimmed the May went on with bird and bower;
The summer filled and faded like a flower:
But rainy Autumn and the red-turned leaf
Found us at tears, and wept for company.

X.

THY baby, too, the child that was to be,
Thro' happier days,—a brightening sun above,—
Held to thy heart with more forgetful love,—
So proud a portion of thyself and me:
We talked it o'er,—the bliss that was to bless;　　　　5
The birth, the baby robes, the christening,
And all our hearts were carried in this thing.
Cold, cold she lies where houseless tempests blow;
The baby's face is here, almost a woe;
And I, so seared in soul, so sapped and shrunk,　　　　10
Gaze hopeless,—careless, in my changed estate
To fall at once, or in the wilderness
Stand like a charred and fire-hardened trunk,
To break the axe's edge of Time and Fate!

XI.

STILL pressing through these weeping solitudes,
Perchance I snatch a beam of comfort bright,—
And pause, to fix the gleam, or lose it quite,
That darkens as I move, or but intrudes
To baffle and forelay: as sometimes here,　　　　5
When late at night the wearied engineer
Driving his engine up through Whately woods,
Sees on the track a glimmering lantern-light,
And checks his crashing speed,—with hasty hand
Reversing and retarding. But, again!　　　　10
Look where it burns, a furlong on before!—
The witchlight of the reedy river-shore,
The pilot of the forest and the fen,
Not to be left, but with the waste woodland.

XII.

HOW most unworthy, echoing in mine ears,
The verse sounds on!—Life, Love, Experience, Art,
Fused into grief; and like a grief-filled heart,
Where all emotion tends and turns to tears,
Broken by its own strength of passion and need: 5
Unworthy, though the bitter waters start
In these dim eyes, reviewing thought and word;
The high desire, the faint accomplished deed;
Unuttered love and loss,—and feverish
Beatings against a gate for ever barred.   10
Yet over and again I range and read
The blotted page, re-turning leaf and leaf;
And half-believe the words are what I wish,
And pore upon my verse, and court my grief,—

XIII.

EVEN as a lover, dreaming, unaware,
Calls o'er his mistress' features hour by hour,
Nor thinks of simple dress, and humble dower;
But pictures to himself her graces rare,—
Dark eyes, dark lashes, and harmonious hair   5
Caught lightly up with amaryllis flower,
Hæmanthus, eardrop, or auricula:
And deems within wide Nature's bound and law
All to beseem her beauty but designed—
Of pure or proud; nor counts himself too bold   10
To fit her forehead with the perfect gold;
Or round her girlish temples belt and bind
Some lamp of jewels, lovelier than the whole,—
Green diamond, or gem of girasol!

XIV.

THE breeze is sharp, the sky is hard and blue,—
Blue with white tails of cloud. On such a day,
Upon a neck of sand o'erblown with spray,
We stood in silence the great sea to view;
And marked the bathers at their shuddering play   5
Run in and out with the succeeding wave,
While from our footsteps broke the trembling turf.
Again I hear the drenching of the wave;
The rocks rise dim, with wall and weedy cave;
Her voice is in mine ears, her answer yet: 10
Again I see, above the froth and fret,
The blue loft standing like eternity!
And white feet flying from the surging surf
And simmering suds of the sea!

XV.

GERTRUDE and Gulielma, sister-twins,
Dwelt in the valley, at the farm-house old;
Nor grief had touched their locks of dark and gold,
Nor dimmed the fragrant whiteness of their skins:
Both beautiful, and one in height and mould;   5
Yet one had loveliness which the spirit wins
To other worlds,—eyes, forehead, smile, and all,
More softly serious than the twilight's fall.
The other—can I e'er forget the day,
When, stealing from a laughing group away,   10
To muse with absent eye, and motion slow,
Her beauty fell upon me like a blow?—
Gertrude! with red flowerlip, and silk black hair!
Yet Gulielma was by far more fair!

XVI.

UNDER the mountain, as when first I knew
Its low black roof, and chimney creeper-twined,
The red house stands; and yet my footsteps find
Vague in the walks, waste balm and feverfew.
But they are gone: no soft-eyed sisters trip   5
Across the porch or lintels; where, behind,
The mother sat,—sat knitting with pursed lip.
The house stands vacant in its green recess,
Absent of beauty as a broken heart;
The wild rain enters; and the sunset wind   10
Sighs in the chambers of their loveliness,
Or shakes the pane; and in the silent noons,
The glass falls from the window, part by part,
And ringeth faintly in the grassy stones.

XVII.

ROLL on, sad world! not Mercury or Mars
Could swifter speed, or slower, round the sun,
Than in this year of variance thou hast done
For me. Yet pain, fear, heart-break, woes, and wars
Have natural limit; from his dread eclipse   5
The swift sun hastens, and the night debars
The day, but to bring in the day more bright;
The flowers renew their odorous fellowships;
The moon runs round and round; the slow earth dips,
True to her poise, and lifts; the planet-stars   10
Roll and return from circle to ellipse;
The day is dull and soft, the eave-trough drips;
And yet I know the splendour of the light
Will break anon: look! where the gray is white!

XVIII.

AND Change, with hurried hand, has swept these scenes:
The woods have fallen; across the meadow-lot
The hunter's trail and trap-path is forgot;
And fire has drunk the swamps of evergreens!
Yet for a moment let my fancy plant   5
These autumn hills again,—the wild dove's haunt,
The wild deer's walk. In golden umbrage shut,
The Indian river runs, Quonecktacut!
Here, but a lifetime back, where falls to-night
Behind the curtained pane a sheltered light   10
On buds of rose, or vase of violet
Aloft upon the marble mantel set,—
Here, in the forest-heart, hung blackening
The wolf-bait on the bush beside the spring.

XIX.

AND faces, forms, and phantoms, numbered not,
Gather and pass like mist upon the breeze;
Jading the eye with uncouth images,—
Women with muskets, children dropping shot;
By fields half-harvested, or left, in fear   5
Of Indian inroad, or the Hessian near;
Disaster, poverty, and dire disease.
Or from the burning village, through the trees,
I see the smoke in reddening volumes roll;
The Indian file in shadowy silence pass,   10
While the last man sets up the trampled grass;
The Tory priest declaiming, fierce and fat;
The Shay's-man, with the green branch in his hat;
Or silent sagamore, Shaug, or Wassahoale!

XX.

O HARD endeavour, to blend in with these—
Deep shadings of the past, a deeper grief;
Or blur with stranger woes a wound so chief,—
Though the great world turn slow with agonies!
What though the forest wind-flowers fell and died,   5
And Gertrude sleeps at Gulielma's side?
They have their tears, nor turn to us their eyes:
But we pursue our dead with groans, and cries,
And bitter reclamations, to the term
Of undiscerning darkness and the worm;   10
Then sit in silence down, and brooding dwell,
Through the slow years, on all we loved, and tell
Each tone, each look of love, each syllable,
With lips that work, with eyes that overwell!

XXI.

LAST night I dreamed we parted once again;
That all was over. From the outward shore,
I saw a dark bark lessen more and more,
That bore her from me o'er the boundless main;
And yearned to follow: no sense of mystery   5
Fell on me, nor the old fear of the sea;
Only I thought, "Knowledge must bring relief;"—
Nor feared the sunless gulfs, the tempest's breath,
Nor drowning, nor the bitterness of death!
Yet while, as one who sees his hope decay,   10
And scarcely weeping, vacant in my grief,
I on the jetty stood, and watched the ship,—
The wave broke fresher, flinging on my lip
Some drops of salt: I shuddered, and turned away.

XXII.

PUT off thy bark from shore, tho' near the night;
And, leaving home, and friends, and hope, behind,—
Sail down the lights! Thou scarce canst fail to find,
O desolate one! the morning breaking white;
Some shore of rest beyond the labouring wave: 5
Ah! 'tis for this I mourn: too long I have
Wandered in tears along Life's stormy way,
Where, day to day, no haven or hope reveals.
Yet on the bound my weary sight I keep,
As one who sails, a landsman on the deep,   10
And, longing for the land, day after day
Sees the horizon rise and fall, and feels
His heart die out,—still riding restlessly
Between the sailing cloud, and the seasick sea.

XXIII.

SOME truths may pierce the spirit's deeper gloom,
Yet shine unapprehended: grand, remote,
We bow before their strength, yet feel them not;
When some low promise of the life to come,
Blessing the mourner, holds the heart indeed,   5
A leading lamp that all may reach and read!
Nor reck those lights, so distant over us,
Sublime, but helpless to the spirit's need
As the night-stars in heaven's vault! yet, thus,
Though the great asterisms mount and burn   10
In inaccessible glory,—this, its height
Has reached; but lingers on till light return,
Low in the sky, like frosty Sirius,
To snap and sparkle through the winter's night.

XXIV.

EACH common object, too,—the house, the grove,
The street, the face, the ware in the window,—seems
Alien and sad, the wreck of perished dreams;
Painfully present, yet remote in love.
The day goes down in rain, the winds blow wide.   5
I leave the town; I climb the mountain-side,
Striving from stumps and stones to wring relief;
And in the senseless anger of my grief,
I rave and weep; I roar to the unmoved skies;
But the wild tempest carries away my cries!—   10
Then back I turn to hide my face in sleep,
Again with dawn the same dull round to sweep,
And buy, and sell, and prate, and laugh, and chide,
As if she had not lived, or had not died.

XXV.

SMALL gossip, whispering at the window-pane,
Finds reason still, for aught beneath the sun:
Answers itself ere answer shall be none,
And in the personal field delights to reign,—
Meting to this, his grief; to that, his gain;   5
And busy to detract, to head or hang!
Oh! wiser far, for him who lieth hid
Within himself,—secure, like him to stay,
Icesius' son; who, when the city rang,
Knew there was news abroad, nor wondered what!—   10
If these conspire, why should I counterplot?
Or vex my heart with guessing whether or not
John went to church, or what my neighbour did
The day before, day before yesterday?

XXVI.

YET from indifference may we hope for peace?
Or in inaction lose the sense of pain?
Joyless I stand, with vacant heart and brain,
And scarce would turn the hand, to be, or cease.
No onward purpose in my life seems plain: 5
To-day may end it, or to-morrow will;
Life still to be preserved, though worthless still,
A tear-dimmed face glassed in a gilded locket.
But Conscience, starting, with a reddening cheek,
Loud on the ear her homely message sends!   10
"Ere the sun plunge, determine; up! awake!
And for thy sordid being make amends:
Truth is not found by feeling in the pocket,
Nor Wisdom sucked from out the fingers' end!"

XXVII.

BUT the heart murmurs at so harsh a tone,—
So sunk in tears it lies, so gone in grief,
With its own blood 'twould venture, far more lief,
Than underprize one drop of Sorrow's own,
Or grudge one hour of mournful idleness.   5
To idle time indeed, to moan our moan,
And then go shivering from a folded gate,—
Broken in heart and life, exheredate
Of all we loved! Yet some, from dire distress,
Accounting tears no loss, and grief no crime,   10
Have gleaned up gold, and made their walk sublime:
So he, poor wanderer in steps like theirs,
May find *his* griefs, though it must be with tears,
Gold grit and grail, washed from the sands of Time.

XXVIII.

YET sometimes, with the sad respectant mind,
We look upon lost hours of want and wail,
As on a picture, with contentment pale;
And even the present seems with voices kind
To soothe our sorrow, and the past endears: 5
Or like a sick man's happy trance appears,
When on the first soft waves of Slumber's calm;
And like a wreck that has outlived the gale,—
No longer lifted by the wrenching billow,
He rides at rest; while from the distant dam, 10
Dim and far off, as in a dream, he hears
The pulsing hammer play,—or the vague wind
Rising and falling in the wayside willow;
Or the faint rustling of the watch beneath his pillow.

XXIX.

How oft in schoolboy-days, from the school's sway
Have I run forth to Nature as to a friend,—
With some pretext of o'erwrought sight, to spend
My school-time in green meadows far away!
Careless of summoning bell, or clocks that strike, 5
I marked with flowers the minutes of my day:
For still the eye that shrank from hated hours,
Dazzled with decimal and dividend,
Knew each bleached alder-root that plashed across
The bubbling brook, and every mass of moss; 10
Could tell the month, too, by the vervain-spike,—
How far the ring of purple tiny flowers
Had climbed; just starting, may-be, with the May,
Half-high, or tapering off at Summer's end.

XXX.

YET, even mid merry boyhood's tricks and scapes,
Early my heart a deeper lesson learnt;
Wandering alone by many a mile of burnt
Black woodside, that but the snow-flake decks and drapes.
And I have stood beneath Canadian sky,   5
In utter solitudes, where the cricket's cry
Appals the heart, and fear takes visible shapes;
And on Long Island's void and isolate capes
Heard the sea break like iron bars: and still,
In all, I seemed to hear the same deep dirge;   10
Borne in the wind, the insect's tiny trill,
And crash and jangle of the shaking surge;
And knew not what they meant,—prophetic woe?
Dim bodings, wherefore? Now, indeed, I know!

XXXI.

MY Anna! when for thee my head was bowed,
The circle of the world, sky, mountain, main,
Drew inward to one spot; and now again
Wide Nature narrows to the shell and shroud.
In the late dawn they will not be forgot,   5
And evenings early-dark, when the low rain
Begins at nightfall, though no tempests rave,
I know the rain is falling on her grave;
The morning views it, and the sunset cloud
Points with a finger to that lonely spot;   10
The crops, that up the valley rolling go,
Ever towards her slumber bow and blow!
I look on the sweeping corn, and the surging rye,
And with every gust of wind my heart goes by!

XXXII.

OH for the face and footstep! woods and shores!
That looked upon us in life's happiest flush;
That saw our figures breaking from the brush;
That heard our voices calling through the bowers!
How are ye darkened! Deepest tears upgush   5
From the heart's heart; and, gathering more and more,
Blindness, and strangling tears,—as now before
Your shades I stand, and find ye still so fair!
And thou, sad mountain-stream! thy stretches steal
Thro' fern and flag, as when we gathered flowers   10
Along thy reeds and shallows cold; or where—
Over the red reef, with a rolling roar—
The woods, thro' glimmering gaps of green, reveal,
Sideward, the River turning like a wheel.

XXXIII.

ONE still dark night, I sat alone and wrote:
So still it was, that distant Chanticleer
Seemed to cry out his warning at my ear,—
Save for the brooding echo in his throat.
Sullen I sat; when, like the night-wind's note,   5
A voice said, "Wherefore doth he weep and fear?
Doth he not know no cry to God is dumb?"
Another spoke: "His heart is dimmed and drowned
With grief." I knew the shape that bended then
To kiss me; when suddenly I once again,   10
Across the watches of the starless gloom,
Heard the cock scream and pause; the morning bell,
Into the gulfs of Night, dropped One! the vision fell,—
And left me listening to the sinking sound.

XXXIV.

MY Anna! though thine earthly steps are done;
Nor in the garden, nor beside the door,
Shall I behold thee standing any more,—
I would not hide my face from light, nor shun
The full completion of this worldly day.   5
What though beside my feet no other one
May set her own, to walk the forward way?
I will not fear to take the path alone;
Loving, for thy sake, things that cheer and bless,—
Kind words, pure deeds, and gentlest charities.   10
Nor will I cease to hold a hope and aim;
But, prophet-like, of these will make my bread,
And feed my soul at peace; as Esdras fed
On flowers, until the Vision and the glory came!

XXXV.

NOR all of solemn is my thought of her:
Though changed and glorified, must there not be
Place still for mirth, and innocent gayety,
And pure young hearts? Or do we gravely err,
And is their happiness too deep for joy?   5
It cannot be: the natural heart's employ
Pours praise as pure as any worshipper
Lost in his rite; too raptured to be gay!
Yes; and such service in its flight outstrips
The cries of suffering hearts that wail and bleed,   10
The groans of grief, wrung from some bitter need.—
This is the faith I bear; and look indeed
To hear her laugh again,—and feel her lips
Kiss from my brow the heavy thoughts away.

XXXVI.

FAREWELL! farewell, O noble heart! I dreamed
That Time nor Death could from my side divorce
Thy fair young life, beside whose pure, bright course
My earthy nature stationary seemed;
Yet, by companionship, direction took,   5
And progress, as the bank runs with the brook.—
Oh! round that mould which all thy mortal hath,
Our children's, and about my own sere path,
May these dim thoughts not fall as dry and vain,
But, fruitful as March-dust, or April rain,   10
Forerun the green! foretell the perfect day
Of restoration,—when, in fields divine,
And walking as of old, thy hand in mine,
By the still waters we may softly stray!

———————

AS Eponina brought, to move the king,
In the old day, her children of the tomb,
Begotten and brought forth in charnel gloom,—
To plead a father's cause; so I, too, bring
Unto thy feet, my Maker, tearfully,   5
These offspring of my sorrow; hidden long,
And scarcely able to abide the light.
May their deep cry inaudible, come to Thee,
Clear, through the cloud of words, the sobs of song,
And, sharper than that other's, pierce thine ears!   10
That so, each thought, aim, utterance, dark or bright,
May find thy pardoning love; more blest than she
Who joyful passed with them to death and night,
With whom she had been buried nine long years!

THE END.

Sonnets. PART III.

I.

Once on a day, alone, but not elate
I sat perusing a forgotten sage,
And turning hopelessly a dim old page
Of history, long disus'd, & out of date:
Reading "his Method" till I lost my own;   5
When suddenly there fell a gold presage
Of sunset sunshine on the letters thrown.
The day had been one cloud, but now a bird
Shot into song; I left my hermitage
With happy heart; but ere I reach'd the gate   10
The sun was gone, the bird! & bleak & drear
All but an icy breath the balsams stirr'd:
I turn'd again, & entering with a groan
Sat darkly down to Dagoraus Whear.

II.

But Nature in her mood, pushes or pulls
At her caprice; we see what is not shown
By that which we behold: nor this alone;
To commonest matters let us fix a bound
Or purport, straight another use is found   5
And this annihilates & that annuls.
And every straw of grass, or dirt, or stone,
Have different function from the kind wellknown
Commerce & custom, dikes & watermills.
Not to the sea alone, from inland earth   10
The stream draws down its freight of floats & hulls,
But backward far, upwinding to the north,
The River gleams, a highway for the gulls
That fly not over land, into the hills.

III.

Yet not for him lifts the low weather cloud,
Not for his solace comes the clearing gale,
Who dreams but on himself: whose breath may fail
And leave no crown his due, no god his debtor:
Of his own gloom, sole builder & begetter;   5
But Nature for thy mirth shall laugh aloud
O trustful child, who on her heart hast lain
In every flow of storm & fit of rain!
So let the day be wilder, windier, wetter,
It irks not thee, nor bids thy fealty end,   10
Affection wasted, & allegiance vain;
But rather seems like an embracing Friend
Who puts thee from him, but to view thee better,
And better so to fold thee close again.

IV.

Thin little leaves of wood fern, ribb'd & tooth'd,
Long curv'd sail needles of the green pitch pine,
With common sandgrass, skirt the horizon line
And over these the incorruptible blue!
Here let me gently lie, & softly view   5
All world asperities, lightly touch'd & smooth'd
As by his gracious hand, the great Bestower.
What though the year be late? some colours run
Yet thro' the dry, some links of melody.
Still let me be by such, assuag'd & sooth'd   10
And happier made, as when, our schoolday done
We hunted on from flower to frosty flower,
Tatter'd & dim, the last red butterfly,
Or the old grasshopper molasses-mouth'd.

V.

How well do I recall that walk in state
Across the Common, by the paths we knew:
Myself in silver badge & riband blue,
My little sister with her book & slate.
The elm tree by the Pond, the fence of wood   5
The burial place that at the corner stood
Where once we cross'd thro the forbidden grate!
The stones that grudgd us way, the graveside weed
The ominous wind that turn'd us half about.
Smit by the flying drops, at what a speed   10
Across the paths, unblest, & unforgiven
We hurried homeward when the day was late
And heard with awe that left no place for doubt
God's anger mutter in the darken'd heaven.

VI.

I look'd across the rollers of the deep,
Long land-swells, ropes of weed, & riding foam,
With bitter angry heart: did I not roam
Ever like these? & what availeth sleep?
Or wakefulness? or pain? & still the sea   5
Rustled & sang, "Alike! & one to me!"
Ay! once I trod these shores too happily,
Murmuring my gladness to the rocks & ground:
And while the wave broke loud on ledge & reef,
Whisper'd it in the pause: like one who tells   10
His heart's dream & delight! & still the sea
Went back & forth upon its bar of shells,
Wash'd & withdrew, with a soft shaling sound,
As though the wet were dry, & joy were grief.

VII.

O rest divine! O golden certainty
Of Love! when Love's half smile illumining pain,
Bade all bright things immutable remain.
Dreaming I stand, the low brook drawling by,
Her flowerlike mien, her mountain step to mark!   5
Ah, I recall when her least look again
Could mar the music in my happy mind
And plunge me into doubt: her faintest sigh
Stir all the fixed pillars of my heaven,
Commingling them in mist & stormy dark!   10
And all together, as I have seen the rain
When the whole Shower is swinging in the wind,
And like a mighty pendulum, urg'd & driven,
Beat back & forth between the earth & sky!

VIII.

As one turn'd round on some high mountain top
Views all things as they are, but out of place,
Reversing recognition, so, I trace
Dimly those dreams of youth & love, & stop
Blindly: for in such mood, landmarks & ways   5
That we have trodden all our lives & know,
We seem not to have known, & cannot guess.
Like one who told his footsteps over to me
In the opposite world: & where he wander'd thro'
Whilst the hot wind blew from the sultry North,   10
Forests that give no shade, & bottomless
Sands, where the plummet sinks as in the sea!
Saw the sky struck by lightning from the earth,
Rain salt like blood, & flights of fiery snow.

IX.

But into order falls our life at last,
Though in the retrospection jarr'd and blent.
Broken ambition, love misplaced or spent
Too soon, & slander busy with the past:
Sorrows too sweet to lose, or vexing joy.   5
But Time will bring oblivion of annoy,
And Silence bind the blows that words have lent;
And we will dwell, unheeding Love or Fame
Like him who has outliv'd a shining Name:
And Peace will come, as evening comes to him,   10
No leader now of men, no longer proud
But poor & private, watching the sun's rim;
Contented too, to fade as yonder cloud
Dim fades, & as the sun fades, fades alike, like dim.

X.

Sometimes I walk where the deep water dips
Against the land. Or on where fancy drives
I walk & muse aloud, like one who strives
To tell his half shap'd thought with stumbling lips;
And view the ocean sea, the ocean ships,   5
With joyless heart: still, but myself I find,
And restless phantoms of my restless mind;
Only the moaning of my wandering words,
Only the wailing of the wheeling plover!
And this high Rock, beneath whose base the sea   10
Has worm'd long caverns, like my tears in me:
And hard like this I stand, & beaten & blind
This desolate rock with lichens rusted over
Hoar with salt sleet, & chalkings of the birds.

XI.

Long Island! yes! when first my vision swept
Thy far faint shores, with inlet & lagoon:
Or misty woodflats where the senses swoon
As in that land where Christian sank and slept,
I thought of him: & then when in the rain   5
We reach'd the Inn; but when I heard them speak
Of Fire Place at hand, & Devil's Neck,
And Good Ground, & Mount Sinai west away,
As in a dream I seem'd to tread again
The Pilgrim's steps, & trace the Heavenly Way!   10
But there sat Happy Jack, with dumb Rejoice,
Red Ike the hostler with his whistling voice,
And an old man I call'd Legality,
Craftily quaint, the tale he told to me.

XII.

"Young Silas Long, a carrier thro' these woods,
Drove home one night in not the best of moods:
Having just seen, a drown'd man flung ashore
With a strange feather cap: & once before
When he was hauling seine in Southold Bay,   5
About this time of year,—a seaman's corse
Wash'd up: with such a cap, & such a face,
And it had brought misfortune on the place.
Pondering he drove: when lo! across the way
He saw, too late, that there a Body lay: 10
Felt the wheels tilt, but could not stop his horse
Or not at once: then, flinging with a slap
The old cloth cover down, he call'd a cap,
Ran back, ten steps or more, & nothing found.

XIII.

Yes! the dead pines & deersfoot on the ground!
So quick return'd again, in five or six:
His cap was gone! & in its stead thrown down,
The very loon-skin the twice-drown'd had on!
With bits of seaweed sticking to the flix!   5
So Long rode home, of cap & sense bereft,
But still can show the dead man's that was left,
And the webs crawl, he says, when the sea rolls!"
Then he, having told his tale & said his say,
By way of emphasis, or corollary,   10
Spat a torpedo in the bed of coals.
"And what! what! what!" squeal'd Ike "became of Long's?"
But the old man here rose & reach'd the tongs,
Laid fire to his pipe & phew'd away.

XIV.

An Episode! yet with a relish rank
Of wild sea places, or of life indeed:
Where yet we find unstirr'd the secret seed
Of song or story marvellous, & thank
The sailor for his jest & manners rude.   5
More welcome too, the old fashion'd fireside
The beach of Devils Aprons at low tide,
Than scandal bleeding-new, or journal dank.
Here, did my dreaming childhood, listening brood
On tales of wind & shipwreck: journeyings made   10
Island or inland: peaks at sea descried
Shap'd like a wave, a table, or a tooth;
Old Peter Batte, that should be Pitherbooth
Gibraltar's, or the grim Rock of Visgrade.

XV.

But we are set to strive to make our mark
And scarcely pause to plead for any play,
Nor think, that any hour, of any day,
Writes its own record down, in chalk or chark,
For all we falsely claim, or blindly say,   5
"I am the Truth! the Life too! & the Way!"
It stands, a Word to comfort & appal,
A summons grave & sweet, a warning stark!
But death & dread responsibility
I hardly fear tonight, or feel at all: 10
Watching my fancy gleam, now bright, now dark,
As snapping from the brands a single spark
Splits in a spray of sparkles ere it fall,
And the long flurrying flame that shoots to die . . .

Sonnets. PART IV.

I.

Still, like a City, seated on a height
Appears my Soul, & gather'd in her place:
Whilst faintly hovering, swarm about her base
Still nearer drawing with the nearer night,
Dim cloudlike groups of men & groups of horse;   5
Outposts & riders of some mightier Force
That lies along the hills: while from them thrown
Rise shadowing shafts, with storms of summoning stone
And the bolt falleth where the crossbolt fell;
Till Doubt contends with Hope, & Fear conspires   10
To thwart them both: so that the Soul retires
Even to her inmost keep & citadel;
And views along the horizon darkening far,
Vague tumult, lights of wo, & moving war.

II.

But Thought, like a mail'd warder helm'd & tall
Treads ever on the outward battlement:
Striving to pierce thro' embrasure & rent
The secret of the gloom that girdleth all.
The immeasurable gulf & interval!   5
Nor heeds the random showers about him sent—
But whilst the cloudy squadrons tramp & wheel,
Busy with weight, & bar, & implement,
He casteth where to make his missiles fall;
Training his engine now, now lower, now higher   10
As a strong archer sets his bow of steel!
Yet some may pass like meteors to the mark,
Of those blind ventures loos'd into the dark
So swift the arrow flies, it taketh fire!

III.

And thus the Mind by its own impulse deep
As lightning instantly enlighteneth,
May cleave the shades of sin, the shapes of death
That pace it round all day, & never sleep,
That watch the wall all night & pace it round,   5
Yet not its own: in man's extremity
God lends the light we use, the strength we keep:
So let us use that light, that we may be
Oh! not perhaps with others, thron'd & crown'd
But at the last in white arrayment found!   10
So daily use it, that the mystery
Of life we touch, in cloud & wind & tree;
In human faces that about us dwell,
And the deep soul that knoweth heaven & hell.

IV.

Yes! pray thy God to give, whate'er thou art,
Some work to be by thee with reverence wrought:
Some trumpet note obey'd, some good fight fought,
Ere thou lay down thy weapons & depart.
Brood on thyself, until thy lamp be spent;   5
Bind all thy force to compass & invent;
But shun the reveries of voluptuous thought
Day-musings, the Floralia of the heart,
And vain imaginations: else, may start
Besides the portals of thy tower or tent,   10
Rending thy trance with dissonant clang & jar
A summons that shall drive thee wild to hear!
Loud, as when in the dreaming Conqueror's ear,
Antigenidas blew a point of war!

V.

Yet some there be, believers for the nonce,
Who God's commands unwelcomely obey;
Lost in the path, they keep the heavenward way
But trip at absolute heaven, & drop at once
In the red gulf: not so, do thou essay   5
To snatch the splendour, & to see the thrones!
Take patience! hope! nor miserably mourn;
If ill enureth, yet abides the good.
Even now, could we look where the white ones wait
Nigh before God; & for a moment scan   10
The angelic faces: even though we stood
In audience of their voices: could we learn
More, than tis love that lifts us near their state,
And the dear fellow aid of man to man.

VI.

And two I knew, an old man & a boy,
Alternate helpers: for their day was spent
In gathering forest bark; & when they went
Late home, the elder did his time employ
To teach the other, & tell him what he knew   5
Of history, myth, or mathematics hard,
In hours of night; & when the night was dark
Show'd him Job's Coffin, & the Golden Yard!
Show'd the nine moonstars in the moonless blue,
And the great Circle of the Bestiary.   10
So that the child grew up to love the sky,
And in the woods beyond the hemlock bark
To heed the intricate moss that o'er it grew,
The shadowy flower, all wet with all day dew.

VII.

But War his overturning trumpet blew!
And in that scattering blast, the knot was rent
That held them: one his faint steps northward bent,
The younger the blind lot of battle drew;
And all seem'd well,—no cause for tears or joy   5
But tidings came, or else of these in lieu
A written word: a hand though rough to see,
The old man lov'd, for he had taught the boy.
At length all ceas'd: the last one *was* the last;
But still he read, & with a fond belief   10
Weigh'd each, as 'twere to find some link or clue:
It never came,—but days the old man past
Pondering upon the letters wistfully,
Silent, & with the fiery eye of grief.

VIII.

Nor strange it is, to us, who walk in bonds
Of flesh & time, if Virtue's self, awhile
Gleam dull like sunless ice: whilst graceful Guile
Blood-fleck'd like hæmatite, or diamonds
With a red inward spark, to reconcile   5
Beauty & Evil seems; & corresponds
So well with Good, that the mind joys to have
Full wider jet & scope: nor swings & sleeps
Forever in one cradle wearily!
Like those vast weeds that off d'Acunha's isle   10
Wash with the surf, & flap their mighty fronds
Mournfully to the dipping of the wave:
Yet cannot be disrupted from their deeps
By the whole heave & settle of the sea.

IX.

Here, where the red man swept the leaves away
To dig for cordial bark or cooling root,
The wayside apple drops its surly fruit.
Right thro' the deep heart of his midmost wood
Thro' range & river & swampy solitude,   5
The common highway landward runs today,
The train booms by with long derisive hoot:
And following fast, rise factory, school & forge.
I heed them not: but where yon alders shoot,
Searching strange plants to medicine my mood—   10
With a quick savage sense, I stop: or stray
Thro' the brush pines & up the mountain gorge:
With patient eye, & with as safe a foot,
As though I walk'd the wood with sagamore George.

X.

Hast thou seen revers'd, the Prophet's miracle?
The worm, that touch'd, a twig-like semblance takes?
Or hast thou mus'd what giveth the craft that makes
The twirling spider at once invisible?
And the spermal odour to the barberry flower?   5
Or heard the singing sand by the cold coast foam?
Or late in inland autumn groves afar
Hast thou ever plucked the little chick-winter-green star
And tasted the sour of its leaf? then come
With me betimes, & I will show thee more   10
Than these, of Nature's secrecies the least.
In the first morning, overcast & chill
And in the day's young sunshine, seeking still
For earliest flowers, & gathering to the east.

Sonnets. PART V.

I.

But Nature where she gives, must give in kind;
Grant to the rich & from the poor withhold;
And much that we in manifest behold,
Is faint to some: while other some still find
Truths that to our sense may be veil'd and furl'd,   5
Publish'd as light, notorious as wind.
But the old Mother moves about her fire
Replenishes its flame & feeds the world;
And so fulfils her births & offices;
Causal or consequential, cares not she,   10
Or ortive or abortive: her desire
Is but to serve, & her necessity.
The invention & authority are His,
In the whole Past, or what remains to be.

II.

Nor, though she seem to cast with backward hand
Strange measure, sunny cold, or cloudy heat,
Or break with stamping rain the farmer's wheat:
Yet in such waste, no waste the soul descries
Intent to glean by barrenest sea & land.   5
For whoso waiteth, long & patiently,
Will see a movement stirring at his feet:
If he but wait, nor think himself much wise.
Nay, from the mind itself, a glimpse will rest
Upon the dark: summoning from vacancy   10
Dim shapes about his intellectual lamp:
Calling these in, & causing him to see;
As the night-heron wading in the swamp
Lights up the pools with her phosphoric breast.

III.

And yet tonight, when summer daylight dies
I cross'd the fields against the summer gust:
And with me, rising from my feet like dust,
A crowd of flealike grasshoppers, like flies;
Presaging dry & dry: continuance, yet   5
Where they prefigure change, all signals must
Fail in the dry, when they forebode the wet.
I know not! all tonight seem'd mystery,
From the full fields that press'd so heavily,
The burden of the blade, the waste of blowth: 10
The twinkling of the smallest life that flits,
To where, & all unconsciously he sits,—
My little boy, symbolling eternity,
Like the god Brahma with his toe in his mouth.

IV.

But man finds means, grant him but place & room,
To gauge the depths, & views a wonder dawn:
Sees all the worlds in utmost space withdrawn
In shape & structure like a honeycomb:
Locates his sun, & grasps the universe.   5
Or to their bearings bids the orbs disperse.
Now seems to stand like that great angel girt
With moon & stars: now sick for shelter even,
Craves but a roof to turn the thunder rain!
Or finds his vaunted reach & wisdom vain,   10
Lost in the myriad meaning of a word:
Or starts at its bare import, panic-stirr'd;
For Earth is earth, or hearth, or dearth, or dirt,
The sky heav'd over our faint heads, is heaven!

V.

Where will the ladder land? who knows? who knows?
He who would seize the planet zone by zone
As on a battlemarch, for Use alone?
Nor stops for visionary wants & woes
But like the Bruce's, on! his heart he throws   5
And leaves behind the dreamer & the drone?
Great is his work indeed, his service great,
Who seeks for Nature but to subjugate:
Break & bereave, build upward, & create;
And hampering her, to carry, heave, & drag,   10
Points to results! towns, cables, cars & ships!
Whilst I in dim green meadows lean & lag:
He counts his course in truth by vigorous steps,
By steps of stairs, but I add crag to crag.

VI.

Licentiate of the schools, with knowledge hot,
A stranger hither came, our dames to frighten:
Who talk'd to us of Christ, the Sibyl's Grot,
Glanc'd at Copernick, though he knew him not,
And show'd us hell; & where the blest abide   5
"The stars" he said, "that round the Northstar glide
For *there* is heaven! tell nightly, as they brighten!"
"But do they move?" I said, "or is it so?"
He answer'd tranquilly, "We see they do!"
It was enough! the crowd was satisfied,   10
And I was hush'd: yet felt my colour heighten.
Was he a knave? a coxcomb? or a clown?
Who stooping thus, our ignorance to enlighten,
Ended by so illuminating his own?

VII.

That night the town turn'd out & cramm'd the Hall!
And I, perhaps maliciously, made one
To hear the lecture: I, who went to none,
And an old friend with me who went to all.
But vain it were that thesis to recall,—   5
A rant of phrase & metaphor: blunder'd thro'
And meaning not: or how, when ended quite
And poetry had clos'd what prayer begun,
Strong men were touch'd to tears! & bright lips grew
Breathless with praise! but my companion   10
Spoke not, or spoke with satire grave & arch;
"We scarce, had had such learning & such light
Since he, the Yankee schoolmaster, last March
Came from Nine Partners to Illyria down."

VIII.

A garden lodge, shut in with quaintest growth,
A slender girl with still kine pasturing near,
And bright look half-expectant, need I fear
Thus to recall that morning when we both
Rode on to the wide City, loud & drear?　　　　　5
Yes, in the shock & tumult hurrying here,
Let me remind thee of that place of peace:
The maiden's smile, the look of happy doubt!
Nor in the stream of things, do thou too, fail
Still to remember me of more than these:　　　　　10
The little valley hidden in the pine,—
The low built cottage buried in the vale,
Wooded and over-wooded, bush'd about
With holm tree, ople tree, & sycamine.

IX.

For these, my friend! were but the foldings fair
The furling leaves about the jewel-flower;
The shade that lent her beauty half its dower,
The beauty that made rich, the shadow there:
Touching all objects with transfiguring power!　　　　　5
The housedog at the door, the village school,
The village in the hills, the hills of Ule!
And thou, Aurania! with thy brow of pearl,
So lov'd from all the world: dids't overrule
All time, all thought, in thy sweet kingdom, girl!　　　　　10
Thro' the slow weeks my fancy found but her,
And day by day, at dusk & dawn-break cool:
All the long moonlight nights I dream'd of Ule,
And in the dark half of the month, my heart was there.

X.

A poet's moonshine! Yes, for Love must lend
An ear to Reason, though tis bitter breath:
Better wild roses died their natural death,
Than evilly, or idly them to rend.
The girl was fair, as flower the moon beneath   5
Gentle & good, & constant to her friend;
Yet out of her own place, not so complete:
Was wedded to her kind—had leave to lack,
But old associations rarely slip:—
Tight as a stem of grass within its sheath   10
You yet may draw & nibble: touch the sweet
With the tip tongue, & browse the tender end,
Half-vacantly: but not to be put back,
Or swallow'd in, but sputter'd from the lip!

XI.

Another! opposite as sky & lands—
As distant too, thy beauty gleams on me:
Bend downward! from thy heaven of chastity
And I will reach with earthy flickering hands!
For I am grim & stain'd. Thou, white & shrin'd!   5
Tis better so! no common love our doom,
Half-nurs'd, half-forc'd, in common cold & gloom:
But quick, convulsively, our souls shall strike
And in the dance of life, tumultuous wind
Like fresh & salt indeed! O! thus may we   10
Join instantly, like to the cloud & sea
In whirling Pillar! nor meet in darkness like
Stalactite & stalagmite, ignorantly
Nearing each other, slow & of one kind!

XII.

'Twas granted:—but the bitter god of Love
As in revenge for some disparagement,
Left us to strive, inextricably blent,
Before we knew in truth, for what we strove:
Or why we went, unwillingly who went,   5
Or whither driven, or who he was that drove.
The countless haps that draw vague heart to heart,
The countless hands that push true hearts apart—
Of these we nothing reck'd, & nothing knew.
The wonder of the world, the faint surmise,   10
The clouded looks of hate, the harrowing eyes;
But pierc'd & pinn'd together! 'twas one to us
With the same arrow smitten thro' & thro,
We fell, like Phædimus & Tantalus!

XIII.

A wash of rippling breath that just arrives,
Thin yellow tufts shattering & showering down:
And underfoot, & all about me blown
Thin yellow tufts & threads, bunches of fives;
Too curiously I note each lightest thing.   5
But where are they? my friends, whose fair young lives
Gave these dead bowers the freshness of the spring?
Gone! & save tears & memory, all is gone!
Fate robs us not of these, nor Death deprives.
But when will Nature here, new beauty bring?   10
Or thou, behold those faces gathering?
I mark the glimmering moss that yet survives,
I touch the trees, I tread the shedded shives,
But when will come the new awakening?

XIV.

And me—my winter's task is drawing over
Though night & winter shake the drifted door:
Critic or friend, dispraiser or approver,
I come not now, nor fain would offer more.
But when buds break, & round the fallen limb   5
The wild weeds crowd in cluster & corymb:
When twilight rings with the red robin's plaint,
Let me give something, though my heart be faint,
To thee, my more than friend! Believer! Lover!
The gust has fallen now, & all is mute—   10
Save pricking on the pane the sleety showers,
The clock that ticks like a belated foot,
Time's hurrying step, the twanging of the hours:
Wait for those days, my friend! or get thee fresher flowers!

XV.

Let me give something! though my Spring be done,
Give to the children, ere their summer time:
Though stirr'd with grief, like rain let fall my rhyme
And tell of one whose aim was much: of one
Whose strife was this, that in his thought should be   5
Some power of wind, some drenching of the sea;
Some drift of stars across a darkling coast.
Imagination, Insight, Memory, Awe,
And dear New England nature first & last!
Whose end was high, whose work was well-begun: 10
Of one, who from his window look'd & saw
His little hemlocks in the morning sun,
And while he gaz'd, into his heart, almost
The peace that passeth understanding, past.

XVI.

Let me give something! as the years unfold,
Some faint fruition, though not much my most;
Perhaps a monument of labour lost.
But Thou, who givest all things, give not me
To sink in silence, sear'd with early cold!   5
Frost burnt & blacken'd, but quick fire for frost!
As once I saw at a houseside, a Tree
Struck scarlet by the lightning, utterly
To its last limb & twig; so strange it seem'd,
I stopp'd to think if this indeed were May,   10
And were those windflowers? or had I dream'd?
But there it stood, close by the cottage eaves,
Red-ripen'd to the heart: shedding its leaves
And autumn sadness on the dim spring day.

Ode.
for the Greenfield Soldiers Monument

This slender spire of glossy stone
   A nation's Emblem poised above,
Speaks it to bleeding hearts alone?
   Ensign of sorrow and of love?

Or here upon this village green   5
   In half-light of the autumn day,
Meet we to mourn for what has been,
   A tale, a triumph pass'd away?

Yes more,—our gift is generous
   As theirs who gave their lifeblood free,   10
Not to the dead alone, to us
   Ourselves, and ours that yet shall be,

We consecrate for distant years—
   No idle rite, our deep hearts stirr'd
And tenderly, with prayers and tears—   15
   The gleaming Shaft! the Eagle bird!

The Shore.

Again from the woods to the shore,
To the edge of the world where the world is all behind
Like the limit of life and death;
Where the wind is an opiate balm, and the soul shall remember
    her griefs
With a dull content at last, and dream and dream.   5

The wind blows in from the shore
The fresh salt smell of the weed, with the briny shells
And my heart tides to and fro:
For here were the lips so loving, here, the hands that
    press'd into mine
With a happiness like pain, for love, for love!   10

I see the hills of the shore,
And above them a belt of the ocean dark and still,
And my eyes come full with tears;

For the white sand hills of the shore, and the shore, and the
    high blue sea,
Bring back my grief but never my joy, my joy.   15

'Twas here we staid by the shore
So late, that the lights on the waters began to move,
The Beacon to glare and go.
For we said, that the day should be dear, come weal, come wo,
    come boot, come bale,
O dear, forever and ever, to us, to us!   20

Alone, at night on the shore
I stand, while the stormy Beacon flares and fades,
And look for that lost delight;
But the rising ridge far out, the shock of the landing billow,
The bitter backward wash, is all, is all.   25

An Incident

Twas in the Country's darkest hour of fear,
Perplexity and peril; overawed
The world hung breathlessly, at home and near
Were bitter foes and bitterer friends abroad,
Nor hope there seem'd beneath the hearse of heaven.   5
On such a day of doubt, and silently
We walk'd apart, the Englishman and I,
Thro' low flat woods that as we rose, rose higher.—
A man he was, expatriate and self-driven
Beyond the deep: adrift, he cared not whither,   10
Hating his land and also hating ours:
In many things lacking the gift to see,
And rating all he loved not, rogue or liar,
Either of both, perhaps, or both in either.
Loving not man, but yet humanity.   15
Loving the white Truth as a boy his bride.

Loving the sun, the ground, the growth, the showers
Believing too, in God and destiny,
And in the general uselessness of life.

"Behold!" (at length he spoke) "the brother strife   20
Is well nigh ending now, and what betide
The country is no more, her Flag is furl'd!
And can it be—that these our foolish eyes
Shall see the close that almost saw the rise?
America the Country of the world!   25
The half-the-world that should have chang'd the whole,
The model flowering of all modern time,
Dropping to pieces like a three days rose?
The rise we saw not, but we see the close
But on the earth no promise of the prime,   30
Nor in the cloud of heaven from pole to pole!"—

"Not so!" I said, "or if so, not so yet:
Our own is ours, and I must first forget
Ere I forego one petal of my Flower,
All happy days and dreams of happy youth;   35
That Spring will come again, that winds will blow.
The early vehement hope, the faith unshaken,
The deep obliging vows our hearts have taken
And once for all, to strike in danger's hour,
And strive and overcome, for Her and Truth!   40
And shall I droop because my Cause is low?
Blood of myself! not so! whilst thou can'st flow
Or give one drop to victory's holy shower!
Still must I deem with him whose precepts say
The darkest hour is just before the day;   45
And if the day be cloud, the land be dearth
He looketh on with far foreshadowing eye,
Sees in the fruitless earth, more fruitful earth,

And in the sky, the sky beyond the sky;
And more and most, in war began the Slave   50
In war must cease, his lifebirth and his grave.
Roll'd as thro' blood the Realm will reach repose,
Cool'd as from fire the clefted land will close;
And battle's field, like a late up-plough'd lot
Return to fresher growths where these are not.   55
No more to hear, our anguish'd hearts will beat,
The midnight raid, the skirmish, the retreat:
All this shall pass,—the smoke shall draft aside,
The kine shall low where late the cannon roared,
And in those vales where now the hurrying sword   60
With blood for sweat, is reaping to the quick,
The farmer shall again his sickle put;—
And where red Strife has stamp'd with angriest stride,
Mid its own orchard-bowers again shall hide
The cottage home with its small children, like   65
The bird's nest set in the print of a horse's foot.

He smiled,—but now a whisper far and sweet
That seem'd to rise again, and faint and flee,
Came to us of the distant mountain breeze:—
He smiled, but answer'd not: and on we wound   70
Still thro the woods, until our weary feet,
Still thro the woods but rising latterly
Gain'd a high place at last above the trees.
A sere and desolate spot; on every bound
Dark woodsides pressing up, and more remote   75
On the land's edge a single parted pinetree.—
"Cans't thou then find" he said "mid outskirts wintry
That golden grace of Spring? thine early creed?
Vows of observance which in youth thou sworest?
Ah! not as now we linger, caring not   80

That life has fail'd with us, half proud indeed
That we have striven, or loved, or suffer'd wrongly,
Firm in despair, or faltering in contrition:"—
Beyond the mountain and the climbing forest,
Beyond the ribs of the far separate pine,   85
Suddenly struck on my averted vision
A single Star thro' twilight twinkling strongly,
A single beam stirring its misty shroud!
Of a world's hope the visible flag & sign
Beneath a single blood bright Stripe of cloud.   90

Poesy

Thou art not fled—
Stunned by the din of this mechanic age;
Nor chilled by wayward stress,
Of wind and cloud to silentness;
Nor in a poet's hermitage,   5
Hidest thy gleaming head;
Though still unwooed thy form the sight evades;
But here amid our glens and dark blue scenery,
And rivulets frilled with fern, and soft cascades,
Rustling down steps of sandstone ceaselessly,   10
And rocks and banks of pines,
Thy solemn beauty wanes and shines;
Have I not seen thee in the river glades?
Or from a mountain gallery leaning down,
Mid depths of green, beheld thy starlike crown,   15
And vaguely caught the wonder of thy song?

While crag and stream and foliaged throng,
Glittered as tinted by the morning's wand:
When the fair West with breath the sense oerpowers,
From orchards blanched with bloom, and all the grassy land,   20
Is dashed with flowers—

Or on a wild hillside
Tanned with the fallen fibres of the pine;
Have I not found thee in the year's decline,
When waste and wide,   25
The winds have shattered October's pride,
In the weak sunshine sitting mournfully? &c—

Twilight

A melancholy eve: the garden walks,
And bowers, & grassy mounds, are dim & damp
And slow commingling in the garden ground;
The whippoorwill sounds faintly from the swamp,
And suddenly dropping boom the twilight hawks: 5
Over the roof the wearied vane goes round
Complaining still, as the wind veers & balks
Its swing: the petals of the cherry tree
Edge the green lawn, & fill each bay & bend
Like the white ruffle of the cold coast foam   10
On some luxuriant shore; from end to end
O'er clumps of lily-flags, & beds of loam
And closing paths, & blackening shrubbery,
The sorrow darkens as they faint & blend.
Their vespers now the marshy choirs begin   15
Tinkling from weedy edge & borders massed

The certain exit of the accomplished day,
And I, though lights & laughter wake within
Darkly oershadowed by the spirit sway
Still linger here, in fitful sadness lost   20
Beneath a Heaven, close sealed with sorrowing gray.

The Cricket

I

The humming bee purrs softly oer his flower,
    From lawn and thicket
The dog day locust singeth in the sun
    From hour to hour:
Each has his bard, and thou, ere day be done   5
    Shalt have no wrong;
So bright that murmur mid the insect crowd
Muffled and lost in bottom grass, or loud
    By pale and picket,
Shall I not take to help me in my song   10
    A little cooing cricket?

II

The afternoon is sleepy,—let us lie
Beneath these branches, whilst the burden'd brook
Muttering and moaning to himself, goes by;
And mark our minstrel's carol, whilst we look   15
Toward the faint horizon swooning blue,
      Or in a garden bower
Trellis'd and trammel'd with deep drapery
      Of falling green:
      Light glimmering thro',—   20
There let the dull hop be
Let bloom, with poppy's dark refreshing flower;
Let the dead fragrance round our temples beat
Stunning the sense to slumber, whilst between
The faltering water and fluttering wind,   25
      Mingle and meet
      Murmur and mix,
No few faint pipings from the glades behind
      Or alder-thicks;
But louder as the day declines,   30
From tingling tassel, blade and sheath,
Rising from nets of river vines,
      Winrows and ricks:
      Above, beneath,
      At every breath;—   35
At hand, around, illimitably
Rising and falling like the sea,
      Acres of cricks!

III.

Dear to the child, who hears thy rustling voice
Cease at his footstep, though he hears thee still,   40
Cease and resume, with vibrance crisp and shrill,
Thou sittest in the sunshine to rejoice!
Night lover too, bringer of all things dark,
And rest and silence,—yet thou bringest to me
Always that burthen of the unresting sea,   45
The moaning cliffs, the low rocks blackly stark.
These upland inland fields no more I view
But the long flat seaside beach, the wild seamew
          And the overturning wave!
Thou bringest too, dim accents from the grave   50
To him who walketh when the day is dim,
Dreaming of those who dream no more of him,
With edg'd remembrances of joy and pain:
And heyday looks and laughter come again;
Forms that in morning sunshine lie and leap,   55
With faces where but now, a gap must be,
Renunciations, and partitions deep,
And closing tears, and crowning vacancy!
And to thy poet at the twilight's hush
No chirping touch of lips with laugh and blush,   60
But wringing arms, hearts wild with love and wo
Closed eyes, and kisses that would not let go!

IV.

So wert thou loved, in that old graceful time
          When Greece was fair,
While god and hero hearken'd to thy chime,   65

    Softly astir
Where the long grasses fring'd Caÿster's lip;
Long drawn, with shimmering sails of swan and ship
    And ship and swan,
    Or where   70
Reedy Eurotas ran.
Did that low warble teach thy tender flute,
    Xenaphyle
Its breathings mild? say! did the grasshopper
Sit golden in thy purple hair   75
    O Psammathe?
Or wert thou mute,
Grieving for Pan amid the alders there?
And by the water and along the hill
That thirsty tinkle in the herbage still,   80
Though the lost forest wailed to horns of Arcady?

V.

Like the Enchanter old
Who sought mid the dead water's weeds and scum
For evil growths beneath the moonbeam cold,
    Or mandrake or dorcynium,   85
And touch'd the leaf that open'd both his ears:
So that articulate voices now he hears
In cry of beast, or bird, or insect's hum,
Might I but find thy knowledge in thy song!
    That twittering tongue,   90
Ancient as light, returning like the years.
    So might I be,
Unwise to sing, thy true interpreter

Thro' denser stillness and in sounder dark
Than ere thy notes have pierced to harrow me.   95
      So might I stir
      The world to hark
To thee my lord and lawgiver,
      And cease my quest;
Content to bring thy wisdom to the world;   100
Content to gain at last some low applause,
      Now low, now lost
Like thine, from mossy stone amid the stems and straws.
Or garden grave mound, trick'd and drest
      Powder'd and pearl'd   105
      By stealing frost,
In dusky rainbow beauty of euphorbias.
For larger would be less indeed, and like
The ceaseless simmer in the summer grass
To him who toileth in the windward field,   110
      Or where the sunbeams strike,
Naught in innumerable numerousness.
      So might I much possess
      So much must yield;
But failing this, the dell and grassy dike   115
The water and the waste shall still be dear,
And all the pleasant plots and places
Where thou hast sung, and I have hung
      To ignorantly hear.
Then Cricket! sing thy song! or answer mine!   120
Thine whispers blame, but mine has naught but praises!
It matters not. Behold! the Autumn goes
      The Shadow grows,
The moments take hold of eternity;
Even while we stop, to wrangle or repine,   125

Our lives are gone,
    Like thinnest mist—
Like yon escaping colour in the tree,
Rejoice! rejoice! whilst yet the hours exist,
Rejoice or mourn, and let the world swing on   130
Unmoved by cricket song of thee, or me.

Notes

Botanical, astronomical, and classical references, along with all other proper nouns, are glossed where they would not be part of a modern educated reader's knowledge (e.g., Erexcéa, chrysolampis, darnels, jacinth) but ignored where they would (e.g., King Arthur, Pegasus, lupine, Sirius). We have noted only a few of Tuckerman's many biblical and literary allusions where they involve verbal echoes rather than proper nouns. All biblical quotations refer to the King James Version. Definitions are quoted where possible from the most recent edition of the Oxford English Dictionary (OED). We give complete citations for our sources where those sources are hard to obtain or otherwise obscure, or else where we quote them at length. Sources quoted by name alone are cited in our bibliography, which follows these notes. Worth noting throughout is the extent of Tuckerman's learning; classical and botanical references, in particular, are often not to be found in the standard reference works of his time, those he seems to have owned (e.g., Lemprière's *Classical Dictionary,* Bigelow's *Florula bostoniensis;* for a partial list of the books in Tuckerman's library, see England, pp. 281–283.

May Flowers.

25   bloodroot: "popular name of several plants, among them Tormentil (*Potentilla Tormentilla*), Crimson Crane's Bill (*Geranium sanguineum*) and Red Puccoon (*Sanguinaira canadensis*)" (OED). Only the second has flowers the color of blood, and only the third is native to North America, though the others have been introduced; the first is reputed to speed the healing of wounds.

Hymn for the Dedication of a Cemetery.

Title   The town of Greenfield dedicated Green River Cemetery in 1851; the extant record of the ceremony refers to no dedicatory poem, only a prayer (by J. G. Willard) and an original hymn (by a Reverend Strong) (F. M. Thompson et al., *History of Greenfield*, vol. II [Greenfield, Mass.: T. Morley, 1904], p. 696).

Infatuation.

20   slav'ry weed: not a sea plant associated with slavery, but (sea) weed surrounded by froth, so that it seems to slaver (as also in "A Soul that out of Nature's Deep," line 175).

Sonnet. ("Again, again . . .")

4   writhled: wrinkled or shriveled (OED).

Picomegan.

Title   The Green River (which joins the Connecticut in Greenfield) was "called by the Indians, Picomegan or the boring river" (D. Willard, *History of Greenfield* [Greenfield, Mass.: Kneeland and Eastman, 1838], p. 19).

70   Yellow-dock and garget: wild flowering plants; garget is also called pokeweed (*Phytolacca decandra*).

Sonnets. ("The starry flower . . .")

5   the Lord of light, the Lamp of shade: that is, the sun and the moon.

Twilight.

49   flags: not banners or pennants, most likely, but one of several leafy creeping plants whose common name is "flag."

To the River.

2   Carro: in modern Italian, "wagon" or "cart," rather than the term of affection "dear" (which has only one r); but Tuckerman must be using the term of affection, from a language whose spellings had not been standardized.

63–65   the Nine: the Muses, to whose number Tuckerman proposes to add a tenth, making them "denary," i.e., ten.

67   chaffering: "Chaffer. To trade, buy and sell, deal in merchandise; to traffic; to bargain, haggle" (OED).

70   Minna more than Brenda: Minna and Brenda are sisters, "two beautiful girls," in Walter Scott's novel *The Pirate* (1822), the latter vivacious, outgoing, and "buoyant," the former "serious" and intimate with nature. "The plants of those wild regions, the shells on the shores, and the long list of feathered clans which haunt their cliffs and eyries, were as well known to Minna Troil, as to the most experienced of the fowlers . . . She had also a high feeling for the solitary and melancholy grandeur of the scenes in which she was placed" (Walter Scott, *The Pirate*, ed. M. Weinstein and A. Lumsden [Edinburgh: Edinburgh University Press, 2001], pp. 21–22).

72   credenda: "Things to be believed" (OED).

91   calypso flower: an orchid commonly known as fairy slipper.

93   Milton or Skelton: i.e., major and minor; dignified and undignified; epic and comic poetry. The English poet John Skelton (d. 1529) is remembered for the speedy, uneven, short rhymed lines now called "skeltonics." Tuckerman may also have in mind the contrast between comic and tragic, gleeful and meditative, modes of life and art in Milton's paired poems "L'Allegro" and "Il Penseroso."

103   delf: delft (fine china).

105–112   Perhaps my hand . . . sacred water: Tuckerman considers, and rejects, involvement in politics: the "Union" is the United States, "polls" voting booths.

115   Golden Bees: presumably the now obsolete folk name for a constellation (compare "Job's Coffin, & the Golden Yard," sonnet IV:VI).

A Soul that out of Nature's Deep.

8   Lyra: the constellation whose name means "lyre," associated with song and poetry; Tuckerman may also have in mind William Wordsworth's deceased Lucy, "Fair as a star when only one / Is shining in the sky."

104   Jesus Christ the Jew: the line must strike a modern ear as an attack on Christian anti-Semites, but it may instead attack uncharitable Christians more broadly (those who do not see God in the least of us); it may even condemn, in the name of Christian orthodoxy, thinkers of Tuckerman's day who denied that Christ was both human and fully divine.

157–159   that warfare . . . the fifth Henry: the Battle of Agincourt, perhaps as depicted in Shakespeare's *Henry V,* or the process of growing into a martial kingship which Shakespeare's Prince Hal (later Henry V) undergoes.

160   Lydiades: or Lydiadas, tyrant of Megalopolis during the Peloponnesian Wars, who "resigned his power, restored liberty to the citizens and joined the city to the Achaean interest" (Plutarch, *Life of Cleomenes,* trans. John Dryden); also described in Polybius and other authors. "Except Cleomenes himself, the later history of Greece presents few brighter names" (William Smith, ed., *A Dictionary of Greek and Roman Biography and Mythology,* vol. II (1870) [New York: AMS, 1967], p. 860).

221–235   All the plants named here are in some way harmful: monkshood, lobelia, fool's parsley, and hemlock are well-known poisons, and darnel (tares) can poison people and cattle, though it also has use in folk medicine. Other plants sting the hands or have a "loathly smell." "Garget" can mean throat inflammation in cows, pigs, or poultry (OED); here as in "Picomegan" it must refer to a plant that, eaten, causes such inflammation.

291   the sailing star: Rigel (also in Orion).

A Sample of Coffee Beans.

8   scarlet runner: not a redcoat or British soldier (as in the OED) but a variety of runner bean, with red flowers; Tuckerman proposes to cultivate these "plain brown beans" alongside the more ornate varieties his garden already contains.

17   As Io fled by Nigris' stream: cf. Ovid, *Metamorphoses,* book I. Transformed into a heifer by Jove, Io fled through the world, falling at last beside the Nile (Nigris), where she prayed that Jove would restore her to human form.

18   brize or bot-bee: a gadfly or bot-fly (OED).

22   amœbæan: "alternately answering, responsive" (OED), as in some classical pastoral poetry. The sense is that poems about beans might be "melodious" even if they conform to no ancient examples, neither those with one speaker, nor with two.

23   banished man: ancient Greeks and Romans spit beans at ghosts.

24   Pythagorean: Pythagoras instructed his disciples to abstain from beans.

38   hemony: or haemony, the imaginary plant in Milton's *Comus* with the power to cancel an enchanter's spell.

39   Ulai: a river in ancient Persia. By its bank the biblical prophet Daniel has a vision (Daniel 8:2).

40   Lote: lotus; here, the food of the mythically indolent lotus-eaters.

56   Canada the Lower: present-day southern and eastern Quebec, including the New England border, was the province of Lower Canada until 1840.

60, 62   Jacko and Poll: standard names for an ape and a parrot.

90   Peto: a minor character, a companion of Falstaff, in Shakespeare's *Henry IV, Part I*.

108   Cow-cliff, Ararat or Api: Cow-cliff is a town in present-day Yorkshire, but Tuckerman may refer to a place name, now lost, in New England; Ararat is the mountain in present-day Armenia where Noah's Ark reputedly came to rest, and Api a peak in the Himalayas—both are mountains mythical and remote, as well as isolated and majestic.

112   vervain dank and chélone: chelone (also called turtlehead) and vervain are wildflowers which might be collected for their medicinal properties.

170   Glaucian traffic: a grossly unequal trade. In book six of the *Iliad* Glaucus exchanges his own golden armor for Diomedes's armor of brass. Tennyson, in his correspondence with Tuckerman, used the same figure for their exchange of pipes (see Introduction; for the complete letter, see Tuckerman, *Sonnets*, p. 28).

171   Homer's shell: a lyre.

172–175   sung in Sapphic . . . the Nine: either Sapphic stanzas, or lyric poetry generally (as against the epic, pastoral and georgic of Homer and Virgil): Tuckerman's digressively comic tale is neither epic, nor lyric, nor georgic or pastoral, and hence might baffle the Nine Muses, who see things in classical terms (though there is a Muse of Comedy, Thalia).

190   Sophi: a wise man, a sage.

213   ale-bench: a bench in or before an ale-house.

Anybody's Critic.

8   five lustrums: twenty-five years.

16   illapse: "to fall, glide or slip in" (OED).

47   the Pied Piper in the Burgelostrassé: properly Burgenstrasse, "Castle Street" or Main Street, along which the Pied Piper of Hamelin would have led rats, as told (among other sources) in Robert Browning's 1842 poem.

52   Pitt and Burke: William Pitt the Elder and Edmund Burke, British statesmen famous for their oratory: the critic prefers political and military ("camp") topics, rather than "brooks, and uplands."

Rhotruda.

Title   The Emperor Charlemagne at first agreed to the marriage of his daughter Rotrud to the Byzantine emperor Constantine VI, in 781, but later reneged, refusing to give Rotrud over to an imperial escort. Henry Wadsworth Longfellow used the same plot for "Emma and Eginardus," a segment from *Tales of a Wayside Inn,* composed (Longfellow's note says) in 1872; Longfellow identifies his source as "the good Monk of Lauresheim . . . in medieval Latin prose," that is, the Latin *Chronicon Laurishamense.* The story has other Latin and vernacular sources in several European literatures. Longfellow himself appears to have used Gabrielle Gaillard's *Histoire de Charlemagne* and Pierre Bayle's famous *Dictionnaire Historique et Critique* (Carl Johnson, "Three Notes on Longfellow," *Harvard Studies and Notes in Philology and Literature* 14 [1932]: 249–271, esp. 271, and Paul Morin, *Les sources de l'oeuvre de Henry Wadsworth Longfellow* [Paris: University of Paris, 1912], p. 638). Bayle, like Longfellow, names the daughter Imma or Emma, but the *Chronicon* does not give the daughter in its story a name.

3   Eginardus: Einhard (c. 770–840), also Eginhard or Eginhardus, the Frankish historian and biographer of Charlemagne, a member of his inner circle, who contributed architectural ideas for the royal palace at Aachen, Charlemagne's favorite estate. Einhard says that Charlemagne let none of his daughters marry, "yet he concealed his knowledge of the rumors current in regard to them, and of the suspicions entertained of their honor" (*Life of Charlemagne,* trans. S. E. Turner [New York: American Book Company, 1880], p. 53).

9–12   regal three: Charlemagne had eight daughters, three by Hildegard: Rotrud, Bertha, and Gisela (Giselia).

58   Pavia's wall: in the Battle of Pavia (773–774) the Franks under Charlemagne besieged and conquered the Lombard (Longobard) capital, Pavia.

86   Fanolehen, or Cunigosteura: tribes under the leadership of Charle-
magne.

94   the Forty: Spengemann and Roberts note that Charlemagne's
attendants were called the Twelve. "The Forty" as a quantity and as a title for
Charlemagne's bodyguards may be an invention of Tuckerman's.

107   cancellate: "Marked with cross lines like lattice-work; reticulated"
(OED).

110   palmirah: "A tall palm . . . with large fan-shaped leaves" (OED).

112–114   Lecœna: or Leaina, or Leaena, the companion (or courtesan) of
Aristogiton and Harmodius, conspirators against the Athenian tyrant
Hippias in the late sixth century BC; she bit off her tongue rather than
betray them. In consequence the Athenians honored a statue of a tongueless
lioness. See Pausanias, *Attica,* I:23.

116–117   Erexcéa . . . anadema: "This said Isle of Lesbos did breed a
second Sappho called Erexcéa, famous in the Art of Poetry, who invented
the Cithern or Rebec and composed many Lyric verses, though she was very
unchaste as several Writers have noted" (André Thevet, "Life of Sappho,"
trans. G. Gerbier, 1657; quoted in *Same-Sex Desire in the English Renaissance:
A Sourcebook,* ed. Kenneth Borris [New York: Routledge, 2004], p. 329). The
name is unusually obscure. An anadema or anadem is "a wreath for the
head, usually of flowers; a chaplet, a garland" (OED; compare "diadem").

119   Uterpendragon: the father of King Arthur.

As sometimes in a Grove.

5   terebinthine: having to do with the terebinth, or with turpentine (the
resin of the terebinth tree); hence bitter, corrosive.

6   grument: viscous, tending to coagulate (not in OED, but compare
"grume" and "grumescent").

24   chrysolampis: the word can denote a tropical hummingbird
(*Chrysolampis mosquitus*), but here it has been imported directly from the
Latin of Agricola, where it denotes an African topaz with "a pale color by day
and a flaming color by night" (Georges Agricola, *De Natura Fossilium,* trans.
M. C. and J. Bandy [1955], p. 128).

48   Levanter: "a strong and raw easterly wind in the Mediterranean"
(OED).

136   Rhodanthe: there is an Australian herb of this name (OED), but
here it must be the invented name of a woman (analogous to "Rhotruda")

whose hand the pilgrim soul would pursue. The Greek roots of the name mean simply "red flower."

175   corallite: a variety of marble (OED).

Mark Atherton.

Title   The tale, the man Mark Atherton, and the woman Bethiah West-brooke all seem to have left no trace in the published record, though there were other Athertons involved in the Indian wars of the late-seventeenth and eighteenth century, described in Epaphras Hoyt's *Antiquarian Researches* (Greenfield, Mass.: Ansel Phelps, 1824) and J. G. Holland, *History of Western Massachusetts* (Springfield, Mass.: Samuel Bowles, 1855); the story may be Tuckerman's invention, or may derive from oral tradition.

26–27   Philip's war and Sassacus . . . De Rouville: King Philip's War (1675–1676) was fought between Native peoples under the Wampanoag sachem Metacom (known to the English as King Philip) and English colonists in southern New England. Deerfield borders Tuckerman's own adopted hometown of Greenfield. "During the long period of the Indian and French and Indian war, Deerfield suffered more, perhaps, than any other town in the commonwealth" (Holland, *History of Western Massachusetts*, vol. II, p. 354). Holland calls the Pequot leader Sassacus, who fought in that war, "a fearless and implacable chief" (vol. I, p. 31); J. H. de Rouville led French, French Canadian, and Indian forces on a bloody attack at Deerfield in 1704. More than fifty colonists were killed, and more than one hundred forced on a months-long trek to Quebec.

99   martin-box: "a nest-box for martins" (OED).

106   River of the Pines: the present-day Pines River runs near Salem, in northeastern Massachusetts, nowhere near Deerfield and Greenfield.

128   peag: wampum.

178   sachem: "supreme head or chief of some American Indian tribes" (OED).

200   Mosely's men: Captain Samuel Mosely led an independent army of volunteers against the Indians in 1675–1676.

204   Winslow, in that desperate day: Josiah Winslow, governor of Plymouth Colony, became commander-in-chief of the forces of the New England Confederation in 1675.

207   abbatis: "a defense constructed by placing felled trees lengthwise" (OED).

Sidney.

51   Deerfield: the Deerfield River, which joins the Connecticut and the Green Rivers in Greenfield.

92–93   Damascus . . . York-and-Lancaster: Damask or Damascus can refer to several cultivars of roses, all pink or red; a York-and-Lancaster rose would be particolored, part white, part red.

Sonnets.

I:I

5   Bloodroot, king-orchis . . . pearlwort: for bloodroot, see note to "May Flowers," above. King-orchis: a type of orchid. Pearlwort: "any of various small tufted or mat-forming plants with inconspicuous white or apetalous flowers, constituting the genus *Sagina*" (OED).

I:II

6   Opposer: Satan.

I:IV

13   stramony: stramonium, thorn-apple, or jimson weed (*Datura stramonium*), or purple stramonium (*Datura tatula*), whose leaves and seeds have narcotic and hallucinogenic properties.

I:IX

13   like Saul: see the sudden conversion of Saul, who becomes the Apostle Paul: he "came near Damascus: and suddenly there shined round about him a light from heaven: And he fell to the earth, and heard a voice saying unto him, Saul, Saul, why persecutest thou me? And he said, Who art thou, Lord? And the Lord said, I am Jesus whom thou persecutest" (Acts 9:3–5). King Saul falls prostrate when the ghost of Samuel tells him that "the Lord . . . shall deliver the host of Israel to the Philistines" (1 Samuel 28:20), but the reference seems less apposite.

I:XI

1   What profits it to me: this sonnet answers (or, in David Seed's view, rewrites) Tennyson's "Ulysses." That poem begins: "It little profits that an idle king . . ." See also Mark 8:36: "What shall it profit a man, if he shall gain the whole world, and lose his own soul?"

I:XII

1   Tall, stately plants: that is, mullein itself, as in line 9.

10   Lion-King: Richard "the Lion-Hearted," King of England, 1189–1199, known for his military prowess; he died in battle.

I:XIV

14   jacinth-flower: hyacinth.

I:XV

2   Oread: "a nymph that inhabits mountains" (OED).

I:XVI

7   other greens ingraft: a realistic description of secondary succession, by which fires leave room for kinds of plants (such as ferns or pine trees) that would not thrive in a mature temperate forest; those plants are then crowded out by shade-tolerant trees.

14   Agria or Artemisia: i.e., bitter and unhealthy drinks; it is better to drink the bitter memory of a "precious-rich" love than simply to drink bitter, and potentially harmful, herbal decoctions. Artemisia are worm-woods; "agria" in a plant's name can simply mean "bitter" (it is a cognate of Latin "amara" and Spanish "amarga"). "Agria plants" in modern usage are desert plants, impossible in New England, while agria grapes are a Hungarian varietal used to make wine.

I:XVII

1–7   All men,—the Preacher . . . differing paths converge: "All go unto one place: all are of the dust, and all turn to dust again" (Ecclesiastes 3:20).

I:XIX

5–8   the Giver . . . pay thee back: compare the parable of the talents (Matthew 25) and Milton's sonnet "When I consider how my light is spent." A sonnet especially rich in biblical allusion.

11   what canst thou: compare God's speech to Job: "Hast thou commanded the morning since thy days?" (Job 38:12).

I:XX

4   pagod, Manada: not a pagoda in the modern sense, but "in South and South-East Asia, an image or carving of a god; an idol" (OED). *Manada*, a Spanish word adopted in the American West, can refer to a group of mares, but that usage makes no sense here: instead, the word means "idol": "At Dabys is another Manada, or idol, no less famous and resorted to: this devil,

or Moloch, is of copper" (W. Johnson, *The Wonders of the Little World*, vol. 1 [London: 1806], p. 368).

8   Bheel: "a central Indian people" (OED); also an alternate spelling of the ancient Near Eastern god Baal, but the parallel with "Greek" requires the former meaning.

14   Ophion: serpent-god, patriarch of the first generation of Titans, in Greek myth as told by Apollonius of Rhodes.

I:XXIII

1   Shall I not see her: the line, and the whole of the sonnet, appears to describe the poet's hopes (as in Milton's "Methought I saw my late espoused saint") for a vision of Hannah beatified after her death; these hopes are satisfied only vicariously, within another "fair young mother's" dream. Golden sees here a description of Hannah, in life, giving comfort to another young mother's grief, an interpretation which seems hard to accept: Golden asserts, incredibly, that the whole of the First Series was "written before 1854" (Golden, pp. 38, 50), a claim evidently based only on the date (1854) inscribed in a notebook where Tuckerman made fair copies (though he may have made the copies years later). England, like almost all other commentators, believes the First Series, like the next four, was written mostly or wholly after Hannah's death (see England, pp. 77, 122).

I:XXIV

11   Manoah's wife: the mother of Samson, who saw an angel (thus answering Manoah's prayer) "as she sat in the field; but Manoah was not with her. And the woman made haste, and ran, and shewed her husband" (Judges 13:9–10).

13–14   Deborah . . . Actia, Arlotte, and Mandané: the prophet Deborah led the Israelites to a military victory (Judges 4); Actia (the mother of Augustus Caesar), Arlotte (the mother of William the Conqueror), and Mandané (the mother of Cyrus the Great of Persia) would all have had prenatal visions of sons' future glory (see Tuckerman, *Complete Poems*, p. xxvii).

II:I

14   poke-berry: "the berry of pokeweed, which yields a red dye; the plant itself" (OED).

II:IV

14   Hephæstian hills: volcanoes, where the Greek god Hephæstus practiced his smith's art.

II:V

7   Cascadnac peak: the Cascadnac is the White River, in Vermont, which joins the Connecticut at present-day White River Junction, but there is no present-day mountain known as Cascadnac; the peak may be Ascutney mountain, in Weathersfield and Windsor, Vermont, considerably south of White River Junction, but also on the Connecticut River.

II:VI

5   perfect grief, like love: "perfect love casteth out fear" (1 John 4:18).

II:VII

3   Hamilcars: either Hamilcar, the general who first organized the Carthaginian army and who was defeated and killed in the battle of Himera in 480 BC, or Hamilcar Barca, the father of Hannibal, the general who from 247–241 BC led the Carthaginians in the First Punic War.

6   florist: either a flower-seller, or a flower-expert, a scholar of flowers, as botanists are scholars of plants.

II:VIII

6   Whippoorwill-shoe, and quaint Sidesaddle-flower: respectively, an orchid, *Cypripedium*, and the common pitcher-plant, *Sarracenia purpurea*, also called Huntsman's Cup.

II:X

1   Thy baby, too: Hannah died of complications from childbirth, but her third child, Tuckerman's youngest son, survived; it is his "face" that Tuckerman contemplates in line 9.

II:XI

7   Whately: a town or village on the Connecticut River in Massachusetts, just south of Greenfield and Deerfield.

II:XIII

7   Hæmanthus, eardrop, or auricula: respectively, blood-flower or African tulip (native to Africa but already cultivated by nineteenth-century American gardeners); fuchsia; and "a species of Primula, also called Bear's ear ... formerly a great favorite with flower-fanciers" (OED).

These choices, which suggest a gardener's care, emphasize the rarity, complexity, and delicacy of her features, by contrast to the "simple dress" of line 3.

14   girasol: "opal which reflects a reddish glow in a bright light"; fire-opal (OED).

II:XVI

4   waste balm and feverfew: medicinal herbs, analgesics, "vague" in the sense that they are no longer deliberately cultivated here: they are Nature's restoratives, not part of a human ameliorative plan.

II:XVIII

8   Quonecktacut: the Connecticut River. The "Indian" spelling occurs on the first text page (p. 4) of Holland's *History of Western Massachusetts* (1855); the telescoped regional history of the following sonnet (II:XIX) suggests that Tuckerman has been reading Holland.

14   wolf-bait: not a flower, but meat left out to attract wolves. The same spot where the house now stands was once so wild that one could trap wolves right there; as in II:XIX and II:XX, Tuckerman allows himself to be carried back many years in time while remaining in just the same place.

II:XIX

6   Hessian: German-speaking mercenaries hired by the British government during the American Revolution.

11   sets up: that is, restores the blades of grass to upright positions, so that the Indians leave no tracks.

13   Shay's-man: a participant in Shays's Rebellion (1786–1787), an uprising against state and national governments: several hundred armed men, led by Daniel Shays, attacked (without success) a federal arsenal at Springfield, and forced the adjournment of courts there and elsewhere in western New England.

14   sagamore, Shaug, or Wassahoale: a sagamore is "the supreme head or chief of some American Indian tribes" (OED). English settlers in 1665 purchased the rights to what is now Deerfield, Massachusetts, from "Chauk alias Chauge, the sachem of Pocomtuck, and his brother Wassahoale" (Joel Munsell, *The Everyday Book of History and Chronology* [New York: D. Appleton, 1858], p. 82).

II:XXIII

10   asterism: "a group or cluster of stars; a constellation" (OED).

II:XXV

9   Icesius' son: Diogenes the Cynic, ancient Greek philosopher, known
for indifference to public events.

II:XXXIII

2   Chanticleer: a rooster.

II:XXXIV

13   as Esdras fed: in the apocryphal book 2 Esdras, an angel commands
the prophet Esdras to go into a field and eat nothing but flowers for seven
days. Esdras follows the angel's instructions and in consequence has a series
of visions culminating in a revelation of the glory of the coming Jerusalem.

II:XXXVII ("As Eponina brought . . .")

1   Eponina: Julius Sabrinus, "defeated in an uprising against the Emperor
Vespasian . . . went into hiding in a nearby cave." His wife Epinone or
Eponina joined him there, "bore twin sons but was forced to keep them
secret"; nine years later, they were discovered by Roman soldiers. After the
Emperor put her husband and sons to death, she insulted him in order to be
killed herself, having no wish to outlive them (Golden, p. 80).

III:I

5, 14   "his Method" . . . Dagoraus Whear: Degory Wheare (1573–1647),
Professor of History at Oxford, author of De Ratione et Methodo Legendi
Historias (1625–1636). "Tuckerman chose this obscure professor," Golden
speculates, "because his name suggests a sense of weariness and because his
book is long forgotten" (p. 82): given the classical and medieval learning
displayed elsewhere in Tuckerman's work, he may also have chosen this
professor because he was actually reading the text, in Latin or in Edmund
Bohun's 1685 translation.

III:V

2   the Common: that is, Boston Common, near where Tuckerman lived
in childhood.

III:XI

4   that land where Christian: the Slough of Despond, in John Bunyan's
Pilgrim's Progress.

7–8   Fire Place . . . Mount Sinai: nineteenth-century place names in
eastern Long Island. Fire Place is the site of modern-day Brookhaven, Good
Ground of Hampton Bays; the town of Mount Sinai retains the name.

III:XII

5   Southold Bay: another place name on Long Island, on the North Fork by the town of Southold. To haul seine is to catch fish by means of a seine, or hanging net.

III:XIII

5   flix: fur (OED); here, the "loon-skin" coat of the deceased man.

11   torpedo: i.e., a cigar.

III:XIV

7   Devils Aprons: "a popular name in the United States of species of *Laminaria* and other olive-brown sea-weeds" (OED).

13   Peter Batte . . . Pitherbooth: perhaps Point of Rocks, in Frederick County, Virginia, "once the seat of the plantation granted in 1642 to Peter Batte," whose Dutch-sounding name might have been pronounced Pitherbooth (Federal Writers Project, *Virginia: A Guide to the Old Dominion* [New York: Oxford University Press, 1956], p. 576). The rock formation that gives the site its name can be seen well only from below, on the south bank of the Potomac River, or from the bridge that crosses the river there; Union troops camped there during the Civil War, and Confederate troops under Jubal Early used the bridge for an unsuccessful raid.

14   Visgrade: i.e., Visegrad, a town in Hungary famous for its high rock, once the site of a medieval fortress and prison; the third in Tuckerman's set of prominent rocks.

III:XV

4   chark: charcoal.

6   "I am the Truth . . . the Way!": "Jesus saith unto him, I am the way, the truth and the life: no man cometh unto the Father, but by me" (John 14:6).

IV:I

1   City, seated on a height: "Ye are the light of the world. A city that is set on a hill cannot be hid" (Matthew 5:14). The phrase, taken from the Sermon on the Mount, has particular resonance in New England, thanks to John Winthrop's 1630 sermon "A Model of Christian Charity," though Winthrop's, and Jesus's, sense of extreme visibility may not suit Tuckerman's metaphor (continued in IV:II) of a medieval siege.

IV:IV

8   Floralia: a spring holiday in ancient Rome, hence, for Tuckerman, an occasion for inappropriate (pagan) rejoicing.

13–14   dreaming Conqueror . . . Antigenidas: the ancient musician
Antigenidas or Antigenides, playing martial music at a banquet, so moved
Alexander the Great that the famous conqueror attacked his guests (so
Plutarch in *De fortuna alexandri,* not to be confused with Plutarch's
better-known *Life of Alexander*).

IV:VI

8   Job's Coffin, & the Golden Yard: constellations, respectively a square
within the larger constellation Delphinus and a now obsolete name for
Orion's Belt.

10   great Circle of the Bestiary: the Zodiac.

IV:VIII

10   d'Acunha's isle: the very remote island of Tristan da Cunha in
the south Atlantic (see Introduction). If Tuckerman envisions the Sar-
gasso Sea here, he is several hundred miles off; he may, however, simply
intend the seaweed that might wash up heavily on almost any Atlantic
beach.

IV:IX

14   sagamore George: a sagamore is a sachem or Indian chieftain, as in
II:XIX: "sagamore George" may be Tuckerman's friend Colonel George
Duncan Wells, since the two friends had often explored the woods. Wells
died in battle in 1864; Tuckerman commemorated him in the poem
"G. D. W." (not included in this edition), writing of Wells, "Twas his to
fathom Nature's hoards." A "sagamore George," also called (by the English)
George No-nose, fought in King Philip's War, but this George was active
near present-day Salem and Boston, rather than in western Massachusetts,
and enjoyed a reputation for battle, not for botany.

IV:X

1   Prophet's miracle: the stick that turns into a snake, and then back into
a stick, in Moses's hand (Exodus 4:2–4).

V:I

11   ortive: "of or relating to the rising of a celestial object" (OED).

V:V

5   the Bruce's: Robert the Bruce, the king and military leader who freed
medieval Scotland from English rule.

V:VI

4, 8   Copernick . . . "But do they move . . . or is it so?": i.e., do the stars actually turn in the Heavens, or is it Earth that moves? The traveling lecturer has not read Copernicus and does not understand modern astronomy.

V:VII

14   Nine Partners to Illyria: Nine Partners was a town in Dutchess County, New York; Illyria must have been the name of a village, now scarce in written records.

V:VIII

14   holm tree, ople tree, & sycamine: holly, guelder rose (*Viburnum opulus*), and black mulberry (OED).

V:IX

7–8   hills of Ule! / And thou, Aurania: these proper nouns have befuddled critics. Jonathan Bean calls Ule "apparently an invention," but Golden, relying on a 1952 travel guide, confidently identifies Ule with Ula, a resort village below hills in southeastern Norway (p. 91). Urania is the muse of astronomy, whose "brow of pearl" (i.e., the starry skies; the Milky Way) could indeed promote indifference to earthly time, both when the moon is full and when it is new ("the dark half of the month"). Tuckerman's notebook from the early 1850s does shift its attention from astronomy to botany, two pastimes or passions indeed "opposite as sky & lands" (V:XI), but the rest of sonnets V:IX, X, and XI seems to require a story about two actual women, rather than two kinds of natural history. There was a Fort Aurania on the Hudson at the site of present-day Albany, New York.

V:XII

14   Phædimus & Tantalus: sons of Niobe, killed (by the god Apollo) with "the same arrow."

V:XIII

13   shives: shive: "a particle of husk; a splinter; a piece of thread or fluff" (OED).

V:XIV

6   corymb: a kind of complex flower, with "a flat or slightly convex head" (OED).

V:XV

14   peace that passeth understanding: "the peace of God, which passeth all understanding" (Philippians 4:7); see Introduction.

Ode. for the Greenfield Soldiers Monument

Title   The poem was actually read at the dedication of the monument in 1870; the monument consists of a high column atop which an eagle pounces on serpents who have crept into its nest. One history of Greenfield reprints the ode, "written for the occasion," along with the rest of the program for the 1870 dedication; the ode is not, however, inscribed on the monument itself (F. M. Thompson et al., *History of Greenfield*, vol. 1 [Greenfield: T. Morey, 1904], p. 381).

The Shore.

Title   Another direct response to Tennyson: compare the English poet's famous (and shorter) lyric "Break, break, break."

An Incident

89   the visible flag & sign: as in "The Star-Spangled Banner," the U.S. flag remains visible in the sky during national strife, though Tuckerman sees not the actual, man-made standard (as Francis Scott Key had) but fragments of it in the sunset, in nonhuman nature.

The Cricket

Title   For the complicated textual history, see Note on the Text. The poem is suffused with echoes of William Wordsworth's "Ode: Intimations of Immortality," of John Keats's "Ode to a Nightingale," and of Tennyson's "Tithonus," whose speaker is a grasshopper (rather than a cricket) himself.

33   winrows: windrow: "a row in which mown grass or hay is laid before being made up into heaps or cocks, in which sods, peats or sheaves or corn are set up to be dried . . . or in which dead branches, etc. are gathered" (OED).

38   cricks: crickets.

67–76   Caÿster . . . Eurotas . . . Xenaphyle . . . Psammathe: "Caÿster is the ancient name of a river celebrated by Homer that empties into the Aegean near Ephesus; Eurotas is a Greek river that flows past Sparta; Xenaphyle (or

Xenaphilus) is a Pythagorean philosopher said to have written on music; Psammathe (or Psamathe), whose name in Greek denotes a sandy shore, is one of the 50 Nereides, the gentle attendants of the sea-goddess Thetis; and Plutarch (the source of other Tuckerman allusions) wrote of the death of Pan in *Why Oracles are Silent* . . . Caÿster, Eurotas, Xenaphilus, Psamathe, and, of course, Pan are glossed in the standard reference work of the time, Lemprière's *Bibliotheca Classica.* Tuckerman owned a copy" (Regan, p. 444). Eurotas is also the birthplace of Hyacinth, mentioned in Milton's "On a fair infant dying of a cough." Another Psammathe, "fearing her father's wrath, exposed her infant Linus, whom she had borne to Apollo. When the child was torn to pieces by dogs, Psammathe's grief was so intense that it revealed her as the mother. The songs of mourning for Linus became an annual rite, and Psammathe's dirges became the well-known Linus songs" (Golden, p. 112).

82   Enchanter old: Spengemann and Roberts identify him as Tiresias (p. 445).

98   lord and lawgiver: i.e., the cricket himself; the line deserves emphasis, given prior critics' insistence on Tuckerman's Christian orthodoxy.

Selected Bibliography

Primary

Tuckerman, Frederick Goddard. *The Complete Poems of Frederick Goddard Tuckerman.* Edited and with an introduction by N. Scott Momaday. With a critical foreword by Yvor Winters. New York: Oxford University Press, 1965.

————. *The Cricket.* Cummington, Mass.: Cummington Press, 1950.

————. "The Cricket." Edited by Mordecai Marcus. *The Massachusetts Review* (Autumn 1960).

————. *Poems.* Boston: John Wilson and Son, 1860. "Imperfect Copy," Houghton Library, Harvard University, Cambridge, Mass.

————. *Poems.* Boston: John Wilson and Son, 1860.

————. *Poems.* London: Smith, Elder and Company, 1863.

————. *Poems.* Boston: Ticknor and Fields, 1864.

————. *Poems.* Boston: Little, Brown and Company, 1869.

————. *The Sonnets of Frederick Goddard Tuckerman.* Edited and with an introduction by Witter Bynner. New York: Alfred A. Knopf and Company, 1931.

————. MS Am 1349. Houghton Library, Harvard University, Cambridge, Mass.

Bean, Jonathan, ed. *Three American Poets: Melville, Tuckerman and Robinson.* London: Penguin Books, 2003.

Secondary

Buell, Lawrence. *New England Literary Culture.* Cambridge: Cambridge University Press, 1986.

Donoghue, Denis. *Connoisseurs of Chaos: Ideas of Order in Modern American Poetry.* New York: Columbia University Press, 1984 (1965).

Eaton, Walter Prichard. "A Forgotten American Poet." *Forum* 41 (January 1909): 62–70.

————. *Penguins Persons and Peppermints.* Boston and Chicago: W. A. Wilde, 1922.

England, Eugene. *Beyond Romanticism: Tuckerman's Life and Poetry.* Provo, Utah: Brigham Young University Press, 1990.

————. "Tennyson and Tuckerman: 'Two Friends . . . on Either Side the Atlantic.'" *New England Quarterly* 57, no. 2 (June 1984): 225–239.

Golden, Samuel A. *Frederick Goddard Tuckerman.* New York: Twayne, 1966.

————. *Frederick Goddard Tuckerman: An American Sonneteer.* University of Maine Bulletin, LIV, 12, April 1952 (Studies in English and American Literature 20).

Groves, Jeffrey D. "A Letter from Frederick Goddard Tuckerman to James T. Fields." *Huntington Library Quarterly* 52, no. 3 (Summer 1989): 403–408.

Hollander, John, ed. *American Poetry: The Nineteenth Century.* Vol. 2. New York: Library of America, 1993.

Hudgins, Andrew. "'A monument of labor lost': The Sonnets of Frederick Goddard Tuckerman." *Chicago Review* 37, no. 1 (1990): 64–79.

Lynch, T. Patrick. "Still Needed: A Tuckerman Text." *Papers of the Bibliographical Society of America* 69 (1975): 255–265.

Marcus, Mordecai. "The Poetry of Frederick Goddard Tuckerman: A Reconsideration." *Discourse* 5 (Winter 1961–1962): 69–82.

Momaday, N. Scott. "The Heretical Cricket." *Southern Review* 3 (Winter 1967): 43–50.

Regan, Robert. "Frederick Goddard Tuckerman." In *Encyclopedia of American Poetry: The Nineteenth Century,* edited by Eric Haralson, 440–445. Chicago: Fitzroy Dearborn, 1998.

Seed, David. "Alone with God and Nature." In *Nineteenth-Century American Poetry*, edited by A. Robert Lee, 166–191. Totowa, N.J.: Barnes and Noble, 1985.

Shannon, Edgar, and Christopher Ricks. "'The Charge of the Light Brigade': The Creation of a Poem." Vol. 38 of *Studies in Bibliography*, edited by Fredson Bowers, 6–10. Charlottesville: University Press of Virginia, 1985.

Spengeman, William C., and Jessica F. Roberts, eds. *Nineteenth-Century American Poetry*. New York: Penguin, 1996.

Tuckerman, Bayard. *Notes on the Tuckerman Family*. Boston: privately printed, 1914.

Wilson, Edmund. *Patriotic Gore*. New York: Oxford University Press, 1962.

Winters, Yvor. *Uncollected Essays and Reviews*. Edited by Francis Murphy. Chicago: Swallow Press, 1973.